How to Improve Your Mind

How to Improve Your Mind

Twenty Keys to Unlock the Modern World

James R. Flynn

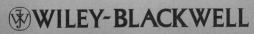

WILEY-BLACKWELL

A John Wiley & Sons, Ltd., Publication

This edition first published 2012
© 2012 John Wiley & Sons, Ltd.

Wiley-Blackwell is an imprint of John Wiley & Sons, formed by the merger of Wiley's global Scientific, Technical and Medical business with Blackwell Publishing.

Registered Office
John Wiley & Sons, Ltd, The Atrium, Southern Gate, Chichester, West Sussex, PO19 8SQ, UK

Editorial Offices
350 Main Street, Malden, MA 02148-5020, USA
9600 Garsington Road, Oxford, OX4 2DQ, UK
The Atrium, Southern Gate, Chichester, West Sussex, PO19 8SQ, UK

For details of our global editorial offices, for customer services, and for information about how to apply for permission to reuse the copyright material in this book please see our website at www.wiley.com/wiley-blackwell.

The right of James R. Flynn to be identified as the author of this work has been asserted in accordance with the UK Copyright, Designs and Patents Act 1988.

Library of Congress Cataloging-in-Publication Data
Flynn, James Robert, 1934–
How to improve your mind : twenty keys to unlock the modern world / James R. Flynn.
    p.   cm
  Includes bibliographical references and index.
  ISBN 978-1-119-94476-8 (pbk.)
1. Critical thinking. 2. Intellect. 3. Knowledge, Sociology of. I. Title.
  BF441.F59 2012
  153.4'3–dc23

                          2012009765

A catalogue record for this book is available from the British Library.

Set in 10.5/13pt Minion by SPi Publisher Services, Pondicherry, India
Printed in Singapore by Ho Printing Singapore Pte Ltd

1   2012

WITH LOVE

To Emily
50 years together

The unexamined life is gross.
(Socrates)

If a nation expects to be ignorant and free,
it expects what never was and never will be.
(Thomas Jefferson)

I have never made but one prayer to God, a very short one:
'O Lord, make my enemies ridiculous.' And God granted it.
(Voltaire)

Contents

Contents

List of Figures and Boxes

Figures

Boxes

Acknowledgments

I want to thank Hetty Marx for her suggestions about organization of the chapters, and Emily Flynn for editing and comments about readability. Bill Dickens was more than generous in giving me tutorials about economics and the crisis of 2008. Needless to say, any mistakes are mine. Dick Nisbett taught me how we "sample" experiences in everyday life. Otherwise, it would never have occurred to me.

Part 1 overlaps with what I said on similar topics in my book *How to Defend Humane Ideals*, University of Nebraska Press, 2000. The same is true of Part 5 and two other books. *Where Have All the Liberals Gone? Race, Class, and Ideals in America*. It is copyright © 2008 James R. Flynn and appears with the permission of Cambridge University Press. *Beyond Patriotism; From Truman to Obama*. It is copyright © 2012 James R. Flynn and appears with the permission of Imprint Academic.

1

Introduction

The Knowledge Trap

Who is to be master, you or the modern world? The world fills your mind from all sides with conversation, lectures, newspapers, TV, and the Internet. You must be the gatekeeper that filters out what is worth remembering and decides what is true or false. Otherwise, you are at its mercy and drift though a life that you manage only day by day. An encyclopedia of facts, and names, and places will not save you. I suspect that the moment you see a term like the naturalistic fallacy (what exactly *does* that mean?) or confounding variable, you stop reading. And if it is clear that an article is a piece of economic analysis, you never start. Unless you have concepts that make you feel confident that you can evaluate what you hear or read, your only defense is to stop listening. How often have you felt degraded because you know you are casting your vote on personalities, rather than a mature evaluation of the government's economic or foreign policy? Even worse is self-deception: we tell ourselves that policies are "socialist" or "reactionary," "imperialist" or "isolationist," even though deep in our hearts we know we are hiding our ignorance behind a word.

I have put my heart into over 50 years of university teaching, at places ranging from Cornell and Maryland in America to Canterbury and Otago in New Zealand. It drives me crazy that there are all these bright young people at universities, and yet, when they graduate, we have not taught them how to think. Despite the scores of lectures and tutorials, the hours of marking and feedback, that I lavished on each of my students, I do not believe I gave them what I value most in thinking my way through life. This book will give you 20 Key Concepts that will empower you to analyze critically what you read, what you hear, and what you see. Without them, your mind does

How to Improve Your Mind: Twenty Keys to Unlock the Modern World,
First Edition. James R. Flynn.
© 2012 John Wiley & Sons, Ltd. Published 2012 by John Wiley & Sons, Ltd.

not have a full tool kit to fashion your own views on ethics, religion, history, economics, international politics, even what you should eat.

I hope I have written it in an accessible style. At times, I speak as if it were directed to those who are disappointed in what they got from their university education. However, some of the most critically aware people I know did not go beyond secondary school and do not intend to do so. If you are one of these, I have not written you off. If you persevere, you will not have the in-depth knowledge or specialized expertise of a graduate of distinguished universities like Oxford and Cambridge, Harvard and Princeton, Toronto and Queen's, Sydney and Melbourne, Auckland and Otago, but you will be able to out-think most of their graduates at that crucial moment when you make up your own mind.

Wherein I Seek Rapport with the Reader

In this book, I will expose you to my own take on the modern world, but I would be most disappointed if I made converts. Everyone who has a critical mind reaches conclusions that other critical minds reject. There is a difference between the *conceptual tools* you need to comprehend the modern world and integrating what you learn into a *comprehensive vision*. Social criticism has led me to views on political economy more palatable to the left than to the right, to the conclusion that religious fundamentalism and postmodernism are enemies of science, and to a perspective on international relations that favors internationalism over nationalism. It would have been "safer" to disguise my vision, but I feel that would destroy your incentive to do critical thinking. What makes it exciting is that it eventually gives you confidence in your ability to paint a picture of the human condition that you can defend.

If we all have a good tool kit, why do we not all agree? Certain beliefs and values are more fundamental than analysis. Assume that two people agree that intelligent design cannot serve as an alternative to the theory of evolution, and that the traditional proofs of God's existence are not valid. One may have a personal faith that he considers authentic, and the other may believe that faith is simply social indoctrination. None of our 20 concepts will unite these two in the sense of making both of them believers or both atheists. Assume two people have the basic tools they need to analyze market behavior, and both agree that providing greater economic equality for the present generation means less economic growth over the next generation. No conceptual tool can unite them if one places a greater value on equality, and the other a greater value on more material progress.

And then there is the fact that you must know things about the modern world to have anything to analyze. Everyone's knowledge will be selective to some degree. Even if you were omniscient, new knowledge comes along that may change your perspective. Take the assumption that greater equality of income and possessions impedes growth. There has always been squabbling about whether this is in fact true in the sense that there seem to be outstanding exceptions, like Sweden, a nation with a high degree of equality and generally high growth. But unless you can say just why equality might promote growth, you are left with argument from brute facts that can be explained away. Sweden may be a special case, small, relatively few immigrants, less ethnic diversity, nothing more than an exception that proves the rule.

After I finished this book, I found a paper from 2006 (what negligence that I had overlooked it) by Sam Bowles (an economist I respect) and Arjum Jayadev (Jayadev and Bowles, 2006). They go beyond brute facts to show why inequality can impede growth, namely, the more unequal a society, the more people are employed in "guard labor." This is a kind of labor that simply supports economic hierarchies in the sense of protecting the power and prerogatives of those at the top and keeping those at the bottom from threatening them. Guard labor is, therefore, unproductive in terms of promoting growth.

They hold that fully 24% of the labor force of America (a very unequal nation) play such a role, ranging from protecting property from those without property (guards, surveillance cameras, those who run the courts and prisons, those in prison, and at times, using troops to quell internal discontent) to supervisors who spend their time ensuring that alienated workers toe the line. I may not fully understand their thesis in that I would have thought that a large proportion of professionals qualify as "guard labor," not just lawyers and judges in criminal cases, but trust lawyers, tax accountants, lobbyists that protect various business interests, and so forth. Clearly, I have some reading to do.

The point is this: a basic grasp of economics (which this book will give you) is a prerequisite for making up your mind on economic policy, but it is not a sufficient condition. You have to expand your knowledge base.

For now, you will have to be content with what one book can offer: 20 tools that will allow you to confront the modern world and begin to construct your own vision. Ninety percent of it is just as relevant for those who reject my peculiar stance as for those who share it, and everyone will be far more able to defend their position after reading it than before. I will try to banish confusions that absolutely prohibit understanding: naive faith in rent, price, and wage controls; appeals to nature in moral argument; rejecting science as merely one point of view among many; and so forth. And best of all, you may gain the confidence that you can think your way through the modern world, rather than be at its mercy.

Key Concepts and Anti-Keys

Over the last century and a half, philosophy, social science, economics, and natural science have enriched our language by giving us some wonderful words and phrases. Each of these stands for a cluster of interrelated ideas that collectively create a method of analysis. I call them "Key Concepts" because they share the property of virtually forcing you to do critical analysis. As someone who has written broadly about controversial issues in ethics, politics, science, the theory of intelligence, race differences in intelligence quotient (IQ), US foreign policy, and even a bit about economics and the history of America's ethnic groups, I have found 15 of them to be indispensable.

There are other concepts that superficially resemble the Key Concepts but are actually wolves in sheep's clothing. They pretend to offer a method of analysis, but the method is either mere words or bankrupt in some other way. I call them "Anti-Keys" because, either by accident or by design, they discourage the use of critical analysis, usually by disparaging science because their users are uncomfortable with it or misunderstand it. I will add five of them to the 15 true keys to make a list of 20. I will list them in the order they appear in the text. For the Keys, I will add the dates they entered educated usage (most dates from the Oxford English Dictionary online), and note the disciplines that invented them. Most of the Anti-Keys are as old as humankind.

Universalizability (1785: Moral Philosophy)

Immanuel Kant first formulated this rule. He thought it could settle virtually all moral questions, but modern thinkers have clarified it and restricted its use. It essentially says that if you state a moral principle, you must stand by it with logical consistency: you cannot praise generosity one day and condemn it the next day (without pointing to some relevant difference).

This makes it sound very humdrum, but you will be surprised how it clarifies moral debate. For example, it puts classical racists in an impossible position. They must say either that they would be subhuman if their skin turned black or that they are superior to black people for some trait like intelligence, which invites evidence to the contrary.

Tautology/Falsifiability (1800: Logic)

We abuse logic when we use it to give a fraudulent defense of something. This is done mainly by deceptive tautologies, that is, statements that appear to be claims about facts but actually banish facts from consideration. Take the claim that the Scots, unlike the English, are a noble people. If you point to a Scot who is a liar and a villain, you may be told, "Ah, he is nay true Scot." The tautology, only good Scots count as Scots, is implicit. The honor of any group can be defended by a definition of the group that excludes the wicked. The Scot in question has used words to define bad Scots out of existence. Nothing counts against the goodness of Scots, which is a cheat.

Karl Popper (1902–1994) used the concept of falsifiability to expose the misuse of tautologies. If anyone makes a claim of fact, ask him what evidence would count against it. If they say nothing, it is just empty words. It is also tempting to misuse the concept of a tautology to discredit something. Darwin's theory of evolution has many enemies. The more sophisticated ones say that it is just an empty tautology, and I will show that they are mistaken. I will also address the naïve enemies of evolution, that is, those who believe in something called intelligent design.

Naturalistic Fallacy (1903: Moral Philosophy)

One should be wary of arguments from facts to values. For example, the mere fact that execution does not deter potential murders (if it is a fact) does not entail that capital punishment is wrong. You may have values (an eye for an eye) that render the fact not decisive.

Tolerance School Fallacy (2000: Moral Philosophy)

Perhaps you have heard someone say, "Do not be judgmental." This makes tolerance the supreme virtue, which is very odd given all the behavior we should not tolerate such as profiting from human misery. There is a fallacious argument that lends such an attitude respectability: it argues that we should respect whatever anyone values because we cannot show that any value is better than another. It makes the attempt to justify your ideals suspect as a supposed source of intolerance. It surfaced in William James, was embraced by anthropologists such as Ruth Benedict, and is now propagated by postmodernists who think they have invented it. Somehow my label for this mistake has not caught on, but no doubt that is merely a matter of time.

Contrary to Nature

This is an "Anti-Key." If you really grasp the naturalistic fallacy, you may be already immune to it. But it deserves analysis because it does so much mischief. By calling something "unnatural," the speaker labels it intrinsically wrong in a way that is supposed to bar investigation of its consequences including beneficial ones. Nature never tells us that something is either right or wrong. It does not condemn gays; we do.

Random Sample (1877: Social Science)

People are often skeptical of a poll because the sample is relatively small. They are mistaken. If the sample is truly random, it does not have to be very large. A random sample is one selected strictly according to chance. If it seems odd that this makes it reliable, note that the only alternative to chance is to introduce a bias. In 1936, the Literary Digest conducted a huge telephone poll that showed that Landon was going to beat Roosevelt for President. However, in those days, few had telephones except the more affluent. The poor were for Roosevelt, and he won in a landslide.

Intelligence Quotient or IQ (1912: Social Science)

In 1905, Alfred Binet published the first modern mental test. In 1912, the German psychologist William Stern introduced the concept of an "IQ." Each child was to be given a score that conveyed whether he or she was typical of children of the same age, or matched the performance of younger or older children. IQ tests may be unpopular today, but I can vouch for the fact that they still determine the fate of many people, ranging from convicts on death row, to those who need a disability benefit, to those who want to be classified as gifted.

Few members of the public fully understand what IQ scores mean, and confusion about their significance is almost universal. IQ scores are significant because they correlate with valuable achievements such as doing well in school. To evaluate them, you will have to learn what a correlation is, and that is founded upon a concept called "regression to the mean."

Placebo (1938: Medicine)

Merely being given a sugar pill (that the patient hopes will work) often relieves the patient's symptoms. A placebo is something that has no beneficial effects aside from those conferred by the subject's faith in it. Without the notion of a placebo, a rational drugs policy would be overwhelmed by the desperate desire for a cure by those stricken with illness.

Charisma Effect (1922: Social Science)

When a technique is applied by a charismatic innovator or disciples fired by zeal, it may be successful for precisely that reason. Patients or students feel that they are being noticed and benefit psychologically, and are spurred on by the excitement of the enterprise.

Control Group (1875: Social Science)

Placebo and charisma effects are special cases of confounding variables. A confounding variable is anything that may blur what you are trying to assess. We introduce an enrichment program in which pre-school children go to a "play center" each day. It is designed to raise the IQ of children at risk of being diagnosed as mentally retarded. Throughout the program, we test their IQs to monitor progress. Assume that at the end of the program, they have higher IQs.

The question arises: what has raised their IQs? Was it really the educational program? Or was it all the others things that were done, such as getting them out of a dysfunctional home for 6h each day, the lunch they had at the play center, the continual exposure to IQ tests. The only way to nullify the effects of confounding variables is to use a control group. You must select a group from the same population and subject them to everything except the enrichment program. Then you may get your answer.

The Sociologist's Fallacy (1973: Social Science)

Sometimes you think you have made a fair comparison between groups, but they are mismatched because they are part of a larger group. For example, you find that the IQs of professionals have dropped from one generation to the next, and you assume that the professions have lost some of their allure (bright people are beginning to prefer other jobs). This ignores the fact that the percentage of professionals has risen dramatically over 30 years. Say it has increased from the top 10% of the population to the top 30%. Well, the top 30% cannot have the same intelligence advantage over the average person as the top 10% does, so the decline in the IQ of professionals may have been precisely because more people wanted to be professionals.

This kind of mistaken matching of groups for comparison is called the *sociologist's fallacy*, which is rather unfair in that sociologists are more aware of it than most academics.

Percentage (1860: Mathematics)

It seems incredible that this important Key Concept made its debut into educated usage less than 150 years ago. The concept of a percentage is an introduction to the closely related concepts of a rate and a ratio. Its range is almost infinite. Recently in New Zealand, there was a debate over the introduction of a contraceptive drug that kills some women. It was pointed out that the extra fatalities from the drug amounted to 50 in one million (or 0.005%), while without it, an extra 1000 women (or 0.100%) would have fatal abortions or die in childbirth. It was heartbreaking how many journalists never got beyond telling their audience that it was a "dangerous" drug.

Market (1776: Economics)

With Adam Smith, this term was altered from the merely concrete (a place where you bought something) to an abstraction (the law of supply and demand). It provokes a deeper analysis of innumerable issues. If the government makes university education free, it will have to budget for more takers. If you pass a minimum wage, employers will find unskilled workers more expensive to hire. They may replace them with machines that employ skilled workers instead. This is not to imply that minimum wage legislation is wrong, but merely that it has to have advantages that outweigh its unwelcome consequences.

Reality is a Text

The phrase behind this Anti-Key comes from Jacques Derrida (1930–2004), but it sums up the anti-science of our time. Those who use it are reluctant to state plainly what it means because its plain meaning is ridiculous: that the physical universe is a blank slate on which we can impose whatever subjective interpretation we like. The evidence against the assertion that all theories are equally explanatory/non-explanatory was refuted every time Derrida put on his spectacles. The theory of optics explained why they worked, and nothing else does so.

This Anti-Key distracts us from what science does (explaining the real world) into the blind alley of classifying the different kinds of texts we "impose" on the world. At its best, it merely copies the distinctions made by orthodox philosophy of science, which is careful to emphasize that some of these "texts" contain truths attested by evidence (physics), while others do not (aesthetic categories). Usually, it blurs these distinctions and asserts that they are all merely subjective, as if the text of an up-to-date telephone book were not more valuable than the text of an out-of-date one *because* it tells the truth about something, namely the phone numbers people actually have. If all of this sounds absurd, that is not my fault.

Alternative Histories

One Anti-Key leads to another. If telling the history of the physical universe is subjective, why should not the history of various peoples be subjective? That is, why should it not be told however they tell choose to tell it, giving us black history, Maori history, and so on. Political correctness gives this notion extra fuel. It was considered demeaning if you told a prescientific people that a scientific approach to its past was more authoritative than their own legends. Legends are not reliable history of any sort, although a real historian may find something that is accurate within them. Each people have their own history, but the methods that best reveal what that history really was are the same.

Alternative Sciences

This Anti-Key introduces confusion because it says that the nature of science varies with who does it (male science, Jewish science). In fact, there is only one scientific method: understanding the universe and human behavior by using theories, predictions based on those theories, and attempts at falsifying those predictions by evidence.

The practice of science is flawed in all the ways in which any human endeavor is flawed, that is, the interests and prejudices of scientists color the

9

problems they investigate, how they go about it, the theories they propose, and the evidence they collect. However, the antidote is better science, not endless and empty assertions that science itself is arbitrary or subjective. The Nazis spoke of Jewish physics as if it was methodologically tainted. It was not: it was simply physics (mainly very good physics) done by Jews. Some feminists have spoken of male science, as if female science was a better alternative. There is no such alternative, although certain women may well do better science than certain men.

Intelligent Design

This Anti-Key tries to use God (or gods) to explain what we see in the physical universe in general and the variety of living things on earth in particular. As a proof of the existence of God, it is no more objectionable than other such proofs. For example, recently it has been argued that the conditions for the development of the universe into something interesting (galaxies, planets, people) require laws so delicately balanced that they could not be an accident but must have been legislated by a creator with an intelligent design. However, intelligent design as an alternative to evolutionary biology is entirely counterproductive. It pretends to be a method of investigating nature that discloses signs of order imposed by a rational agent. In fact, it adds nothing to our knowledge of nature. Whenever science is unable to give a full explanation of something, we get nothing better than a monotonous refrain: "it was designed that way."

The National Interest (1939/1948: Social Science)

If you wanted to understand a person's behavior, you would ask yourself at least three questions. What does his self-interest dictate? Does he always seek his interests, or is he sometimes swayed by friendship (or enmity), and at other times by his self-image, perhaps whether he thinks of himself as unusually virtuous or knowledgeable or both. Modern theories of international relations ask the same questions about nations but have an unfortunate tendency to push one question at the expense of the others.

The concept of the national interest took hold beginning with Carr's (1939/2004) *The Twenty Years Crisis* and Morgenthau's (1948) *Politics Among Nations*. The latter awakens some nostalgia in me in that I took Morgenthau's course at the University of Chicago in 1952. The theory he pioneered was called *realism*, because he argued that the only rational foreign policy was the pursuit of "national interest" taking into account the realities of the balance of power.

To weaken your nation so as to pursue altruistic goals was irresponsible and condemned as idealism. Political realism never monopolized the theory of international relations thanks to the two competing schools that follow.

National Affinities (1939/1917: Social Science)

Liberalism is a theory that holds that the relative power of nations is often less predictive of their behavior than whether or not they have some affinity with one another, that is, shared culture, or are economically dependent on one another, or all have democratic government. The original realists called this particular brand of idealism "Wilsonian idealism." They attributed it to Woodrow Wilson, the US President who was the architect of the League of Nations (parent of the United Nations) at the end of World War I.

National Identity (1989: Social Science)

Constructivism holds that every nation has a unique national identity shaped by its sense of itself, that is, its values, mores, culture, institutions, and history. Nicholas Onuf coined the term in his book *World of Our Making* (Onuf, 1989). That makes three schools of international relations theory. Since each of these schools has a share of the truth, it seems odd that they all did not merge into one, but there is nothing to prevent you from using all three of their basic concepts to get a real understanding of how nations behave.

Box 1.1   Keys replace SHAs

Readers of my book, *What is Intelligence: Beyond the Flynn Effect* (Flynn, 2007/2009), will notice a change in labels. What I once called short-hand abstractions (SHAs) and Anti-SHAs are now called Key Concepts and Anti-Keys.

I call these 20 notions *Key Concepts* because they identify the keys that unlock the door to understanding the modern world, plus naming the anti-keys that do nothing except spread confusion (see Box 1.1)

Universities and the Knowledge Trap

Given that I have spoken of the need for wide-ranging knowledge, it may seem odd to speak of the *knowledge trap*. I will illustrate what I mean by recalling my own experience at the University of Chicago. It prided itself on its great books program, books that exposed all undergraduates to philosophy, history, social science, natural science, the humanities, and so forth. Its faculty had a coherent notion of what an educated person should know and adopted a curriculum that forbade too much specialization. The lecturers were themselves critically aware and made sure that all students were exposed to the concepts they needed somewhere in the collection of courses they took. However, even this university failed to educate properly.

The problem is that every lecturer is commendably eager to impart knowledge, and the Key Concepts get lost in the sheer volume of that knowledge. I am guilty as well. When I teach an introductory moral and political philosophy course, I do discuss the pitfalls of tautologies and the naturalistic fallacy. But there are so many fascinating things to teach about Plato's theory of being, his theory of knowledge, his psychology, and his theory of tyranny. And then there is Aristotle, Hobbes, Marx, and Nietzsche. A colleague teaches history with due emphasis on what distinguishes real history from mere tradition or self-serving myths. But there are the fascinating events that led to World War I, and how the class system structured strategic thinking and made the lives of ordinary soldiers cheap, and why the League of Nations was doomed.

Even if you tell students to note and treasure the Key Concepts as you introduce them one by one, they simply do not stand out from the background of the total content of the course, all of which will be on the examination. The concepts of one course do not appear in the next course, and those encountered in one year are absent the following year. Students would have to keep a special Key Concepts diary, to be compiled and consulted for its own sake, to be added to on the rare occasion when a new concept is encountered, and sustain this as a regular chore throughout their undergraduate experience. What university actually advises this, rewards this, and keeps track of whether it is being done? On one level, the antidote is simple: just prior to graduation, every department should offer its majors a one-semester course that identifies the concepts and shows how to use them.

Substitute for a Diary

This book is a substitute for the diary you never kept at school or university. The concepts fall naturally into five groups: those associated with philosophy, the social sciences, economics, the nature of science, and international politics. The next 18 chapters will present them in that order. By the end, you will have a good tool kit. No doubt, the 20 concepts I have selected reflect my competence. If I knew more about the environment, I would list "Gaia" (the concept of the Earth as an integrated living entity) and "tipping point" (the point at which gradual change suddenly turns into chaotic change). Let others write similar books, but these 20 concepts will do for a start.

References

Carr, E. (2004) *The Twenty Years' Crisis, 1919–1939*, Perennial, New York. (Original work published 1939).

Flynn, J.R. (2007) *What is Intelligence? Beyond the Flynn Effect*, Cambridge University Press. (Expanded paperback edition 2009).

Jayadev, A. and Bowles, S. (2006) Guard labour. Journal of Development Economics, 79, 328–348.

Morgenthau, H.J. (1948) *Politics Among Nations*, Knopf, New York.

Onuf, N.G. (1989) *World of Our Making*, University of South Carolina Press, Columbia, SC.

Part 1
Arguing about Right and Wrong

2

Logic and Moral Debate — Attacks on Blacks

Key Concept: (1) Universalizability. *Logic clarifies all kinds of debate, but its role in moral debate is often overlooked. This is a pity, because it can be a weapon of extraordinary power.*

Preview: *Logic and the rule of universalizability; blacks and blackness; why we must take the hypothetical seriously; abortion and its slogans; the unborn mosquito.*

Ethics consists of judgments about how people ought to behave and how people ought to be treated. Asking whether or not someone's judgments are logically consistent with one another can put them on the defensive. Philosophers call this the "rule of universalizability." Some philosophers try to read into it more than logical consistency, and this engenders a controversy. I will evade it by not doing so.

Blacks and Blackness

Classical racists say that all blacks (or Jews or "even" whites) ought to be treated as inferiors. They should be denied freedom from bondage, the vote, freedom of movement, freedom to marry any partner that is willing, and so forth. The first question that should be put to them is: why? This forces them to state what is called the practical syllogism. They then have a choice, namely, to appeal to sheer blackness of skin or name a desirable human trait for which blacks are supposedly deficient. Assume the first option:

How to Improve Your Mind: Twenty Keys to Unlock the Modern World,
First Edition. James R. Flynn.
© 2012 John Wiley & Sons, Ltd. Published 2012 by John Wiley & Sons, Ltd.

Major premise: All people with black skin should be denied the right to vote.
Minor premise: Thirty-seven million Americans have black skin.
Conclusion: Therefore, those Americans should be denied the right to vote.

If racists choose this option, we can ask what they would say if their own skin turned black, perhaps because we sneaked a pill in their food or because of some pollutant in the water supply. This of course is a demand for logical consistency. In reply, they must answer in the positive or the negative. We can learn much from examining a positive answer.

The penalties are subtle but compelling. To say I should be treated badly simply because I am now black may seem to be a heroic willingness to suffer for one's principles. Actually, it trivializes one's moral principles. It says that I am willing to suffer for an absurdity, namely, that color nullifies personal traits as criteria for assessing human beings. Hitler did not tell the Germans that they were superior simply because they were white or were Aryans; rather he told them that they were more creative, courageous, and commanding than the rest of us. Imagine a Nazi orator telling his German audience that they deserved to be ruled by Africans just because the two groups had exchanged skin colors.

Imagine a book reviewer. He tells his readers to avoid one book because it has a black cover and to buy another because it has a white cover. The next day, he tells them to do the reverse because new editions have reversed the colors. Even racists would give up reading this book reviewer in favor of one who deigned to discuss plot, character, dialogue, and style. If racists grant that it is absurd to ignore the traits of fictional characters when nothing is at stake but a good read, can they seriously contend that we should ignore the traits of real people when the stakes are who has a right to a decent life?

That is why real-world racists choose the second option and assert a correlation between color and despised personal traits:

Major premise: People who are permanently immature in mind and character should not have the right to vote.
Minor premise: All blacks are permanently immature.
Conclusion: All blacks should not have the right to vote.

Once logic has forced them to enter the real world and assert factual hypotheses, falsification by evidence follows automatically. We can point to thousands of counterexamples, the thousands of blacks of genius or talent ranging from Gordon Parks (the great photographer, composer,

18

author, and poet) to Paul Robson (great Shakespearian actor and multi-lingual orator) to Thomas Sowell (great ethnic historian) to Franklin Julius Wilson (great sociologist). The last word belongs to Frederick Law Olmsted. When traveling through the antebellum American south, he found laws against educating blacks defended on the grounds that blacks could no more learn to read or write than animals or maniacs. He asked, why, then, there were no laws on the books forbidding people to teach animals and maniacs how to read.

It may appear that racists have a third option, namely, to restate their principles, so as to save logical consistency. They might say "those with black skin are exempt if they are born at 6 pm on April 28, 1934 and that happens to be my birthday." Philosophers sometimes invent such evasions to show the limitations of the demand for logical consistency. They do not deny that if someone makes a moral judgment, they must apply it to all situations in which the relevant conditions are the same. But they say, how can we possibly agree on what conditions are morally relevant? This racist says his birth date is morally relevant. We can imagine an infinite number of refinements to any moral principle to escape the charge of inconsistency. How can we hope to even state all of these?

It is these refinements that are irrelevant. It is not academic philosophers but racists who must try to escape the charge that they lack consistent principles. They may care nothing for logic. But unless they render their moral judgments consistent, people do not even know what they are buying into if they become racists. If someone praises generosity, and then tells me that his next-door neighbor (whom he may dislike) is wicked, despite the fact that she gives money freely to her friends in need, I am due an explanation: "I thought you admired generosity, but here is a generous person you condemn, just what are your moral principles?" It is he who has an interest in supplying an answer: "Ah, if you only knew her, you would understand that she lacks a generous motive and merely gives to her friends so they will feel indebted to her." And then I find that his neighbor gives even more money anonymously to charity. Is he then to say "but she was born on April 28, 1934, and that disqualifies her from moral approval"?

Well, he can say that sort of thing without violating any rule of logic. But now I know he does not take his own stated principles seriously. If he does not take them seriously, why should anyone else? In fact, neither racists nor anyone who really believe in their principles will trivialize them by "revising" them in a way that turns them into something they do not cherish, much less something they find absurd.

Taking the Hypothetical Seriously

The same is true about taking the hypothetical seriously. People who live in pre-scientific societies may be literal minded and simply say, "but my skin has not turned black and probably never will." However, by refusing to generalize their principles to cover hypothetical situations, they cheat themselves of the opportunity to determine whether their own "principles" are a hodgepodge of inconsistent moral judgments or a coherent moral system. To simply appeal to traditional morality and refuse to generalize is a refusal to use reason. It means that you pay the same price as a stone: you cannot engage in rational discourse. In the modern world, where the number of rational agents is rising, the price of opting out of moral debate is both personal and political. You act on principles you might alter upon reflection; you offer moral principles to others that appear contradictory.

Abortion and Its Slogans

Converting slogans into practical syllogisms would force many to reconsider their position on the ethics of abortion. The opposing sides often use language that obscures the existence of question-begging moral principles. Take those who adhere to a right to life and tell us that abortion is murder. That is not very informative because "murder" means wrongful killing, and the whole debate is about whether abortion is wrongful killing. Presenting the point syllogistically, we get:

Major premise: Some kinds of killing are wrong.
Minor premise: Abortion is that kind of killing.
Conclusion: Therefore, abortion is wrong.

The logic is impeccable, but then so is: some squirrels are wrong, abortion is that kind of squirrel, and therefore abortion is wrong. The minor premise classifies abortion in a way that is debatable. When the person in question says why abortion should be classed as wrongful killing, we get what is really being said: terminating innocent human life is wrong, no matter what the stage of development; abortion terminates innocent human life; therefore, abortion is wrong.

If we deny the moral principle on which the argument is based, we will be asked whether we would act the same in a hypothetical situation that appears similar. If it were convenient for a mother, would we allow her to terminate the life of a child who had just entered a coma that will last nine months? That initiates a real moral debate.

Those who think abortion morally permissible may respond with the slogan that a woman has a right to control her own body, which implies a distinction between a fetus that is in the womb and a child who has begun an independent existence, to which the reply will be, yes that is so, but it is only a prima facie right that can be overridden by more fundamental moral considerations. What if, by not having an abortion, you could save the life of a newborn child that will be in a coma for nine months? This may seem far-fetched, but the real challenge is this: with an innocent life at stake, do you *really* believe that whether the child is inside you or outside you makes a decisive difference?

This is not an unanswerable argument. The obvious response is, imagine that you (and now we are posing a question to males as well as females) are unique in that could save the life of an anonymous stranger, but you can do so only at a price. You would have to come in daily to give blood transfusions for a period of nine months. Early on, these will make you vomit most of your meals. Your normal activities will be increasingly curtailed. At the end, you will be committed to a painful bone graft, and there will be a small risk of losing your life. Once all of this is done, there may be another stranger that you are uniquely able to save under the same conditions.

The argument is far from resolved, but at least it is a proper moral debate. Rather than continuing it (for example: "but you consented to the act that begat this stranger" – "did I, what about rape"), I want to introduce a new point. There is a danger that simply to give yourself a strong position in a debate, you will endorse principles in bad faith.

Very few who believe in a right to abortion feel comfortable in saying that this is an absolute right that persists unaltered up to the moment of birth. Many approve an absolute right to abortion on demand in the first three months of pregnancy but believe that good reasons should be given later on. Perhaps desertion by the prospective father would be good enough until the eighth month, but after that, only a real risk to health. After all, the mother need not raise the child: there are plenty of people who want to adopt. It is not easy to defend a right to terminate life simply because it upsets you to think of "your" child alive elsewhere.

The easy way out of this dilemma is to state a moral principle: a woman has an absolute right of abortion until the time when the child can survive, without great risk of abnormality, outside the womb; thereafter, more and more serious reasons would have to be given. Well, the invention of an effective artificial womb could push that time backwards. If a fetus can survive at one month outside the womb, does that mean the mother has no right over its fate?

If you can answer, "that is exactly what I mean, with all the parents who want to adopt, the fetus should be extracted and kept alive, no matter what her wishes," you are in good faith. If you think this would be an abolition of a woman's right to choose, it shows that you selected a criterion simply because it was convenient, but in which you did not really believe. You should be serious about your moral principles: they define who you really are.

Women and Femininity

Men who wish to deny women a full role in modern society do not simply say, "I hate women." They realize that this would be bankrupt as a reason for differential treatment and, therefore, assert a correlation between femininity and personal traits that are supposed to justify differential treatment. This means that they have satisfied the rule of universalizability but only by paying the usual price: they must defend their correlation against evidence to the contrary. As Russell put it, they must equate femininity with some kind of incurable disease.

It will not do that they find statistical differences between the sexes, such as that more men can lift heavy weights then women. If a job requires strength, they should hire whoever is strong without reference to gender. If they assert that women are more vulnerable and need to be protected by their husbands, let them show that cloistered women are actually better off than single women who have no such protection. Let them offer reasons why women should be forbidden to take whatever risks are entailed by moving outside the home, when men take all kinds of risks to improve their lot.

The Unborn Mosquito

You must also maintain logical consistency as you go from one issue to another. I once supervised a student who was both a keen advocate of animal rights and a feminist. She opposed the spraying of mosquito larvae, even if that was necessary to stop the spread of malaria. That was the thin edge of the wedge: the next step would be to conduct medical experiments on dogs to find cures for illnesses. Admirable consistency. But it raises the question of where she stood on abortion. If it was wrong to kill unborn mosquitoes to save people from death, what about killing unborn human beings just to save a woman from maximizing her welfare? She gave up her thesis to marry a Persian whose restaurant had roast lamb as a specialty.

3

Getting Rid of Tautologies – No Private Clubs

Key Concept: (2) Tautology. *Having looked at the use of logic in moral debate, we now look at its abuse. The concept of a tautology clarifies the roles of logic and evidence.*

Preview: *Tautologies; tautologies pretending to be something else; falsification; tautologies used to include or exclude; is evolution a tautology?*

The best way to introduce the concept of a tautology is to distinguish between two kinds of propositions. Everyone is familiar with geometrical propositions such as "a square has four sides." Sometimes, philosophers call these *analytic* propositions because their truth is guaranteed by logic, that is, if you alter "has four sides" (the predicate), you do violence to the concept of a "square" (the subject). If you call something a three-sided thing, it is not a square but a triangle. They differ from *synthetic* propositions in that the latter connect subject and predicate by experience, such as "a yellow balloon is floating out in the hall." If we want to settle that question, logic is helpless: we have to go out into the hall and look, and our experiences will either verify the proposition or falsify it. If someone denies that a square has four sides, it is not because the proposition is falsified by his experiences. He is probably a foreign-language speaker who has a different word for square than we do.

Philosophers debate whether all propositions can be neatly classified as analytic or synthetic. However, this need not concern us because we will be dealing with clear cases.

How to Improve Your Mind: Twenty Keys to Unlock the Modern World,
First Edition. James R. Flynn.
© 2012 John Wiley & Sons, Ltd. Published 2012 by John Wiley & Sons, Ltd.

Tautologies

Tautologies are analytic in the sense that they are truths guaranteed by logic. But they pay a price for this: they tell us nothing about facts or causes and effects. They need not be trivial or obvious. Much of pure mathematics consists of tautologies. Take the geometry you (hopefully) learned in high school. A proposition like the angles of a triangle equal 180° is a logical truth. If you deny it, sooner or later you will run into a logical contradiction. We say that it is a proposition of pure mathematics rather than applied mathematics because, unlike the equations used in physics, it does not apply to the physical universe. A perfect triangle may have 180°, but that does not tell us that there is anything in the physical universe that has 180°. It may be that no perfect triangle exists except in our minds. "Harvard Square" in Boston, or indeed any city square anywhere, is not a perfect square.

Tautologies Pretending to be Something Else

The nature of tautologies makes it tempting to abuse them: you state them in a way that obscures the fact that they tell us nothing about the real world by using language that appears to refer to the real world. You make them into claims that seem to be about people or events that have all of the certainty of logic and that no one can deny.

Needless to say, these claims protect something you admire from criticism. It is a historical fact that many workers show no signs of a revolutionary psychology and are a conservative influence, such as hard hats that vote Republican, or keep blacks out of the construction trades, or demand subservience from their wives, or hate Mexican immigrants. A Marxist may respond, "but those are not real workers." Instead, he calls them members of the "lumpenproletariat."

Originally, the lumpenproletariat was that sector of the population that, having been denied a legitimate way to make a living, were forced to become thieves, fences, drug pushers, numbers men, gamblers, pimps, prostitutes, loan sharks, beggars, thugs, etc. But extending the term to people who earn their living with their hands and yet do not have a "worker's psychology" provides no answer to the historical question of whether the actual working class is a revolutionary force. You can say that someone who works with their hands is not a real worker unless they live up to your ideal, but now we are getting tautologies rather than history.

The devout sometimes say: "No true Christian has ever been malicious." That is perfectly acceptable so long as they are merely making explicit an ideal: "I believe the core of Christian ethics is charity, and therefore, anyone who does not live up to that is not practicing Christian ethics."

However, it is often used when they have been challenged about the record of Christianity as an historical influence, the slaughter of heretics, the persecution of the Jews, Crusaders and their unprovoked wars against Islam, the follies of Christian missionaries, Priests telling soldiers that their cause is just, the use of the concept of heaven to reconcile the exploited to their lot. To reply, "but they were not true Christians" is to refer to your ideal Christian rather than the people who actually considered themselves Christians and attended Catholic and Protestant churches. You can define your ideals, as you like. Using evidence to defend the proposition that Christian churches have done humankind more harm than good cannot be evaded by a tautology. Its certainty and invulnerability to falsification do not transfer. You must enter into the historical debate and provide a case for the defense (see Box 3.1).

Box 3.1   Reason and faith

Religion often opposes faith to reason, but that is no excuse for sheer bad argument. If you commit yourself to arguing from evidence, the rules of evidence apply. I have recently finished one of those sad books by an intelligent and learned theologian trying to reconcile the benevolence of God with the horrible suffering some people endure through no fault of their own, for example, all of those small children over the centuries who screamed their lives away until a disease or hunger finally killed them.

The argument is that if the God-made world is so bad, why do we not have mass suicide? Aside from the fact that we are now defending God as having principles we can tolerate rather than ones we can admire, there is no admission that the evidence must cut both ways: if one person's failure to commit suicide counts for God, the fact that others have committed suicide counts against him. The best He can get is a majority decision.

The only coherent solution to the problem of evil is that God has a higher morality unknown to us within which justice and humanity are subordinate principles sometimes overridden by others. Believers once had the courage to say this, but today, it makes them uneasy.

Social scientists are not immune: "Alienation is the cause of suicide." When you point to members of a street-corner gang, none of whom have committed suicide, the reply is that they were alienated not from their peer group but from the larger society. If they are kicked out of their gang, the rebuttal is that they had a faithful best friend or lover. If they are totally isolated and do not commit suicide, they must have Asperger's syndrome and, being oblivious to others, do not have a normal need for social support. Although it is never explicitly admitted, it becomes clear that nothing counts against alienation as the cause of suicide. The mere fact you are not prone to suicide shows you are not alienated, and the mere fact someone commits suicide is logically sufficient to class that person as alienated. The possibility of falsification by evidence is not allowed, which is proof that we have cut our ties with the real world.

Falsification

The fact that claims about the real world are at least in principle falsifiable is a powerful tool of analysis. By falsifiable, I simply mean that we can at least conceive of evidence that would show the claim to be invalid. The best example of a confused argument that implodes when we raise the question of falsifiability is a familiar one. I refer to debate about whether all human actions are egotistical. This appears to pose a question about what in fact motivates people. All too often, a tautological argument is offered that claims to settle the questions in favor of egotism, as follows.

We act only on internalized needs or wants. If you seek money, it is because you want to. If you choose to lay down your life for another, you must want to. When the Christians died for their faith in the Roman arena, they would not have done so unless they wanted to, would they? So, all human actions are basically selfish in motivation, and the ethical merit of all is reduced to the common denominator of zero. Whatever action you propose to the psychological egoist is met by the same response. He would not have let himself be tortured to death to save his comrades unless he wanted to.

What seems to be the strength of this argument is actually its Achilles heel. Psychological egotism pretends to be a theory of human motivation. What would one have thought of Newton's theory of astronomy if it were compatible with any event in the heavens whatsoever? The job of a theory is to predict this rather than that, to predict that you will see Mercury here rather than there, not to say, well you might see it anywhere. A good theory may never actually be falsified, but we have no trouble imagining cases that would falsify it. So, psychological egoism is bankrupt as a theory of motivation.

It is really a play on words with a hidden assumption. Unless I am under the spell of a hypnotist, I am autonomous in the sense that I chose to do whatever I do. Psychological egoism calls this choosing "responding to a want," but all that really means is that I act in terms of some value I internalize. What else; who can act on values that someone else internalizes? Some people internalize other-regarding principles and act on them and we say that they have a moral motivation. Others internalize only self-regarding maxims and act on those, and we say that they are selfish and seek only what they want. Other-regarding actions often mean sacrificing my wants in the sense that with a heavy heart, I do my duty even though it causes me great suffering. You can call that doing what I want to do if you wish, but then we will simply distinguish wants sub-1 from wants sub-2: distinguish people who internalize only self-regarding "wants" from those who internalize other-regarding "wants." Most of us call the latter moral principles.

The psychological egoist can assert that other-regarding principles are peculiar in that, unlike other deeply internalized "wants," they are impotent in terms of actually causing human behavior. But now he has entered into the real world and must provide evidence. A wide range of human behavior seems explicable only on the assumption that people care more about the welfare of others than themselves. Something that is not a moral principle may underlie a moral principle of course. All of our internalized values may rest on a bed of brain physiology. So may all of our aesthetic judgments, but nonetheless, we judge some things to be beautiful, and others ugly. After we have done our duty, we may take a certain satisfaction in the fact that we have lived up to our moral principles (if we are sill alive). That merely shows we love the good rather than do it out of a sheer intellectual perception that certain things are good. It hardly drains our actions of moral worth.

Tautologies Used to Include or Exclude

Some tautologies are obnoxious because they seek either to reserve a favorable status to some alone on arbitrary grounds or to grant immunity to some from an unfavorable status on arbitrary grounds.

Take the assertion, often made by human-rights commissioners, that blacks, or some other group that is subject to racism, cannot themselves be accused of racism. If this translates into a tautology, blacks cannot be racists because my definition of racist stipulates that they must be non-black, it is a closed circle of words that makes no contact with reality. You may define roses as non-red. We cannot prevent you from speaking a private language if you want, but the practice is futile. Those of us who want language to describe the real world will humor you by using two labels: "rose" and "things that are like a rose in every way except that they are red." If a black lynches a Chinese boy for dating his daughter simply because he hates Chinese, he is racist in every way except that he is black.

Similar arguments are used to arbitrarily exclude a group from a favored status. Some feminists deny that men can be feminists. Some years ago, at my university, there was a male student whose dedication to the cause of women's rights was extraordinary. The radical feminist group was quite unwilling to call him a feminist, but he drove them crazy. If qualifying meant that you had to picket beauty contests, he was on the picket line. If you had to bite a policeman on the ankle, he would bite a policeman on the ankle.

Now it is perfectly sensible to assert that you have never met a man whose behavior showed that he truly held feminist principles. But whatever criterion you set, both men and women must qualify if they meet it, unless you want to commit the absurdity of saying that only female feminists are feminists. This is on a par with a definition of socialist that stipulates that only gay socialists are socialists. You may predict that men are unlikely to hold feminist principles deeply enough unless they experience what women experience, for example, being raped. But most women have never been raped, so this translates into no man can imagine the horror of rape. That can be falsified. Whenever I hear about homosexual rape in prisons, my horror is lively indeed.

Is Evolution a Tautology?

Sometimes, a summary statement of a theory uses words that make it appear to be a tautology when it is not. Even sympathetic scholars make this mistake about the theory of evolution by saying that "natural selection" is a tautology. The argument: natural selection is about the survival of the fittest; but who are the fittest, why those that survive? It is just a closed circle of definitions and therefore empty words.

I am afraid that the only safeguard against being deceived by such arguments is knowledge about the theory being debated. Natural selection can be described as follows:

- Each offspring is a genetic novelty, that is, it has genes somewhat different from the population of which its parents are a part.
- Offspring occupy much the same environmental niche as their population.
- That niche can only accommodate a population of limited size.
- Therefore, if the genetic novelty of an offspring renders it more likely to reproduce (viable offspring) than the other members of its population, over some generations, its genetic novelty will tend to dominate the whole population.
- If a sufficient succession of genetic novelties occurs, they can constitute the evolution of the population into a new species.
- These novelties are caused by the shuffling of the genes during reproduction (no child looks exactly like either parent) and by random mutations that alter genes.

All of these propositions are significant assertions that can be evidenced and not one of them is merely a tautology.

To think clearly, we must distinguish the facts of evolution from the theory that has been constructed to account for those facts. As with astronomy or any other science, contemporary theory may need to be improved if it is to do its job properly. As set forth above, the theory falls into two parts. Every proposition except the last describes the mechanism of natural selection, the process by which it is decided whose genes shall dominate a population. Up to now, no scientist has found an alternative to natural selection that has its explanatory power, so its status seems secure. But the last proposition describes the "motor" of evolution, that is, the forces that cause genetic novelties. And it claims that random mutations provide them quickly enough to account for the facts, namely, the transition from one species to another that we find in the fossil record. That is very much disputed. Sometimes, the fossil record shows new species occurring so quickly that it is hard to see how random mutations could account for the speed of evolution.

Several alternatives have been suggested, all of which revise the random occurrence of genetic novelties into something more structured or directed:

- When a mutation of one gene occurs, it can affect other genes in a way that produces a sort of functional package, one that can be a radical departure from the past but still have a good chance of survival. In other words, chromosomes have a structure that shapes mutated genes in a felicitous way.
- Certain laws affect all living things and propel mutations into of one of the mathematical possibilities available to life (shades of Plato).
- Species alter radically by borrowing genes from other species.
- Epigenesis – certain adaptations to environment can actually affect genes and be passed on to an offspring "pre-adapted" to prosper in that environment.

All of these bring an element of design into evolution, but they do so in a scientifically fruitful way. We can look for evidence in their favor, rather than positing some mysterious entity that just must have designed living things to be the way they are.

Aristotle's ethics is sometimes falsely labeled a tautology. He is sometimes taken to say that good acts are those approved by good people and that good people are those habituated to do good acts. Nothing could seem more empty and circular than that. In fact, Aristotle states a series of propositions. First, only healthy organs afford reliable experiences – we do not ask someone with an eye disease to look through telescopes. Second, there is a healthy state for the human character that can be known by what way of life gives rise to symptoms of psychic health (which he calls eudaimonia). Third, a life of humane fellow feeling and creative work (preferably contemplative) perfects human character. Therefore, the perfected (rather than the diseased) person should be our standard of right and wrong (we should heed his or her moral judgment). Naturally, the judgments such a person makes will be essentially humane judgments.

None of these three propositions are tautologies. In theory at least, the second and third propositions can be tested against evidence (does a life of humane love and creative work maximize one's sense of well-being?). The first is a proposition about how we obtain knowledge. I believer it is mistaken: if the only people that could see clearly were those who suffered from eye diseases, we would ask them to look through telescopes. But mistaken or not, it must be debated and cannot be dismissed as an empty tautology.

4

The Naturalistic Fallacy and Its Consequences – be Judgmental

Key Concepts: (3) **The naturalistic fallacy**; (4) **the tolerance school fallacy**. *Over the centuries, philosophers have rightly labeled certain moral arguments "fallacies." Despite this many survive and are used almost universally. The two we will discuss are linked and we must be clear about the consequences of recognizing them as fallacies. Otherwise, we will feel unwarranted despair or joy.*

Preview: *The naturalistic fallacy; facts and values; the relevance of facts; the nihilist fallacy; the tolerance school fallacy; the one-way street; the naturalistic fallacy revisited.*

Having stressed the role of logic in moral debate, we now come to an important claim about the limitations of logic, namely, whether logic can leap the gap between facts and values. For example, someone may believe that the *fact* (supposed fact) that capital punishment does not deter potential murderers entails the *value* proposition that we ought to abolish capital punishment. Such people are committing the "naturalistic fallacy."

Some claim that there are exceptions to the logical divide between "is" and "ought." However, none of these exceptions are morally significant. They have not found facts that logically entail moral advice as to what people ought to do, or facts that logically entail holding humane moral principles rather than anti-human ones. Since my chief interest is how you can justify humane ideals against their opponents, I lost interest in the "is/ought" question when the limitations of possible exceptions became clear. After all, the main reason to want exceptions is this: we can use the scientific method to lend objectivity to propositions of fact (Mars

How to Improve Your Mind: Twenty Keys to Unlock the Modern World,
First Edition. James R. Flynn.
© 2012 John Wiley & Sons, Ltd. Published 2012 by John Wiley & Sons, Ltd.

has two moons); if certain facts logically entailed humane values, they would be equally objective.

Facts and Values

If you think that evidence that executions do not deter potential murders is decisive, ask yourself why. The usual answer is because the lives lost on the scaffold are not being matched by other lives saved. This generates a practical syllogism:

Major premise: Anything that costs more lives than it saves is wrong.
Minor premise: Capital punishment costs more lives than it saves.
Conclusion: Therefore, capital punishment is wrong.

There is nothing the matter with the syllogism as it stands. The naturalistic fallacy arises only if you think that the major premise is self-justifying, that is, you believe that the very fact something costs more lives than it saves *logically entails* that it is wrong. This is simply not so. Your principles may evaluate the execution of murderers purely in terms of the consequences for preserving the maximum number of human lives. But others hold different principles: they may believe that the relatives have a right to compensation for the life lost, an eye for an eye; or, like Nietzsche, they may believe that great art flourishes only in societies that have not been "tamed" by the elimination of cruelty, and that great art is more important than anything else. In other words, the connection between the subject (costs more lives than it saves) and the predicate (is wrong) is supplied by your commitment to humane ideals. People who are committed to other moral principles can reject it. You may think them wicked, but they are not committing any logical error.

Most scientists and social scientists do not know any philosophy, and therefore, some commit the naturalistic fallacy. Biologists write books that assume that the fact something is a trend in evolution (the expansion of consciousness, greater awareness of the perspectives of others) shows that it is morally admirable. Social "Darwinists" write books that assume that since there is cut-throat competition for survival among certain species, we ought to maximize economic competition. Awareness that facts alone do not settle moral issues will enable you to identify many examples.

The naturalistic fallacy is unique in that while awareness of it clarifies moral debate, unless its consequences are understood all that clarity is lost in a welter of confusion. The confusions are three: the exile of facts; the nihilist fallacy; and the tolerance school fallacy.

The Relevance of Facts

The naturalistic fallacy does not mean that logic and facts have no role to play in moral debate. When we looked at someone with the values of the classical racist, and forced them to universalize their principles, they were led to say things falsifiable by facts, for example, that all blacks were permanently immature in either intellect or character. There may seem to be a mystery here: certainly if there is no logical bridge between facts and values, there can be no bridge between values and facts.

Logic is not everything. Value inclinations are not enough to give anyone a morality they can live by. You must link your values to the real world by way of certain factual propositions, and these "connecting propositions" can be tested against evidence. Marx may have had a proclivity to admire the proletariat, but he did not just run through the streets shouting, "I love workers." This would have put him on a par with someone who says, "I hate my boss," significant to him perhaps but of little interest to the rest of us. We might meet a Frenchman who goes berserk every time he hears the word "camel." An interesting quirk but not easy to convert into a set of moral principles. What Marx did was clothe his value proclivity with significance by elaborating a theory of history that gave the working class a crucial role in progress toward a humane society. That puts him at the mercy of evidence. As we have seen, some Marxists find the possibility of falsification too onerous to bear, and use a tautology to escape its verdict (the "lumpenproletariat" fiddle).

Similarly, although racists may hate black people and that hatred may be the psychological basis of their ideology, they do not just run through the stress shouting, "I hate the color black." To turn their hatred into more than a quirk, they must connect it to the world by way of assumptions about genetics (race-mixing debases the offspring), history (if only blacks had existed, the human race would never have become literate), human potential (black immigrants will always be a burden on the public purse), and so forth. Lest we feel too smug, our fellow-feeling for humankind is also a mere proclivity until it is connected to the larger world, and it is up to us to make sure we assert no claims that cannot survive the tests of logic and evidence.

Nietzsche challenges us by asking whether any serious person could care about the fate of common people without ignoring their sheer awfulness: the heavy-handed working-class father braying at a female impersonator on TV. The meritocracy thesis tells us that our ideals self-destruct in practice, that is, if we ever got equal environments and perfect social mobility, the result would be a society dominated by a genetic elite (for a refutation, see Chapter 10). Economics tells us that while we may have sympathy for those on low wages, a minimum wage erodes the pool of jobs available for unskilled labor (for a discussion, see Chapter 12).

Just as we demand logical consistency and an honest appraisal of evidence from our opponents, we must make sure our ideals measure up. If you believe in your ideals only because you think every worker noble, or every woman would be perfect unless debased by the company of men, or that all people are basically good, you will not last long in moral debate. Nietzsche asserted that Dickens had never painted a picture of someone who had a "good heart" without describing a fool.

The Nihilist Fallacy

Throughout history, well-intentioned thinkers have tried to find a logical bridge from facts to values, so that they could "demonstrate" that humane ideals are somehow more objective than anti-humane ideals. What could be more objective than founding humane ideals on facts plus logic? That would give our ideals a special status in the light of truth; and the difference between Nietzsche and ourselves would not be "just" commitment to one set of ideals rather than another. With the recognition of the naturalistic fallacy came recognition that there was probably no way of showing that humane ideals had objective status.

In *The Brothers Karamazov*, Dostoyevsky says that if God is dead, anything is allowable. God for him was the only source of knowledge of good, and he meant that if the good was not objective, all moral ideals were trivialized. They collapse into the category of mere whim or desire. Risking one's life to pull a child out of the path of an oncoming car becomes no different from van Gogh's mad whim to cut off his ear. We may be passionately committed to principles that tell us that we should act humanely, but the message of those principles is deceptive. They are like hallucinations whose content deceives.

To put the argument in a syllogism:

Major premise: There is no defensible criterion of objectivity in ethics.
Minor premise: My ideals lack objectivity.
Conclusion: Therefore, I must treat my own ideals as unworthy of regard even from myself.

This argument is logically incoherent and should be labeled the "nihilist fallacy." Commitment to a moral principle is a commitment to a duty, and it is far more serious than a mere preference for one soft drink over another, which no one confuses with a self-imposed duty. In the absence of an ethical truth-test of some sort, a humane person cannot tell Nietzsche he ought to accept humane ideals. However, to say that we ourselves ought to abandon humane ideals is to claim more than that they lack objective status. It is to claim that they have subjective status, that we should discount them as if they were hallucinations. But why do we discount a hallucination? It is because it has *failed* a truth test. It is deceptive about something: we saw an oasis in the dessert, and when we ran to get there, we got a mouthful of sand rather than a mouthful of water.

If there is no test of objectivity in ethics, humane ideals can neither pass nor fail – there is no test to fail. What are they supposed to be deceptive about? They are not deceptive about our deepest selves. In the absence of objectivity, there is no such thing as subjectivity. It may be foolish to say humane ideals ought to be accepted by those who loathe them, but it would be equally absurd to say they ought to be dismissed by those who cherish them.

Let us clarify what objectivity entails, so we can be clear about what ethics is missing. Science is possible because some people's visual experiences (and the propositions of fact they base on their vision) are worthy of regard from others, despite the fact that others may not share those visual experiences. If you and I are standing at the back of a lecture room, and, thanks to astigmatism, you see a blur on the white board at the front while I see a circle, I can make a prediction that will show you that my visual experiences are better "truth-finders" than your own. I can predict that if you walk toward the board, when you get close enough, you too will see a circle. That is because we all live in a shared physical universe.

I do not believe that there is a shared moral reality we can appeal to when people have fundamental conflicts of moral principle. Others as wise as Plato have disagreed, and you should read them before you make up your mind. But if I am correct, we can make no case for objectivity in ethics because there is no truth-test (read those who dispute that as well). We cannot claim that certain ideals are worthy of Nietzsche's regard (that he must value them) no matter whether he has a proclivity towards them, or loathes them, or is indifferent to them. But that does not mean that I cannot be deeply committed to humane ideals and die in the ditch for them if that is necessary. They may not mean anything to Nietzsche, but they mean a lot to me.

The Tolerance School Fallacy

The fact that accepting the naturalistic fallacy cheated humane ideals of their objectivity did not dismay every one. Others treated it as a source of joy, well if not quite joy, as a balm to soothe their souls. That is because they used the collapse of objectivity as a foundation on which to build a new fallacy.

William James (1842–1910) is perhaps America's greatest philosopher. However, he tried to use lack of ethical objectivity as the foundation of egalitarian ethics and thus committed a logical mistake. I will state and criticize James's argument and then examine a debased version of the argument current in America. I call the latter "the tolerance school fallacy" because it is usually used in an effort to justify tolerance, or at least something that is a pale shadow of tolerance.

James's argument can be stated as a syllogism:

Major premise: There is no defensible criterion of objectivity in ethics.
Minor premise: That means we cannot label certain human demands or the demands of certain people as objective, thus putting them ahead of the demands of other people.
Conclusion: Therefore, we should treat all human demands as worthy of satisfaction without reference to what they are or whose they are.

The conclusion implies that we should satisfy as many human demands as possible and not favor our own over those of others, an attractive morality for some. However, the conclusion does not follow because it contradicts the premises.

It is indeed true that the absence of objectivity in ethics means that no human ideals have a special status in the sense that all should treat them as worthy of regard, even though they do not internalize them. But the conclusion tells us that we should treat the demands of others as worthy of regard *whether we internalize their demands or not*. It amounts to asserting that literally every human demand has objective status: mine and thine are on a par, even though I care only about mine.

If we lack a criterion of objectivity in ethics, we can hardly go from saying that certain human demands cannot be labeled objective to saying that all human demands have objective status. Note that this argument is the mirror image of the nihilist fallacy. The latter claimed that lack of a test of objectivity in ethics means that we had to treat all human ideals, including our own, as if they had flunked a non-existent test of objectivity. James is saying that we must treat all humane demands as if they had passed a non-existent test of objectivity.

Most Americans have never read James, but they have an argument that they use to justify tolerance that is similar in its logical structure:

Major premise: All values are culturally relative.
Minor premise: That means we have no reason to favor any values over any others.
Conclusion: Therefore, we have an obligation to be tolerant and treat all values as equally valid.

This argument also self-destructs when it is realized that an obligation to be tolerant is itself a moral principle or value and not something else, say, a turnip. Thus, it too is culturally relative, and, according to the terms of the argument, we have no reason to favor it over intolerance. Some may say that while tolerance is not logically entailed by cultural relativism, it is an obviously appropriate psychological reaction. But actually, the reaction depends on the person: psychology sets no limits on itself. When it breaks free of logic, it can move anywhere from appreciation of diversity and tolerance to disgust for the "primitive" and a sense of arrogant self-approval.

In any event, enough has been said to show that when Americans base their egalitarian ideals on lack of objectivity in ethics, they are building on sand. When tolerance is given preferment over its opposite on the grounds that no one's values merit preferment, something has gone wrong. Tolerance and equality, group chauvinism and elitism, all are values and must share a common fate. The former do not pop out of a pit that has swallowed all values unless a conjuror is at work.

The "ethics of tolerance" should not be confused with a principled defense of civil liberties or free speech, quite the contrary. It often manifests itself as an antipathy to free speech, that is, as anger toward anyone who argues that human societies or groups are different in a way that might imply a value judgment in favor of one over the other. Forbidden topics for debate range from that certain cultural practices are wrong (even female circumcision is supposed to be tolerable), or that white and blacks differ on average in their genetic potential for intelligence. I have spent a good deal of time arguing against the latter, but it enrages me that honest scholars who differ are howled down, at universities of all places, by staff and students, as if that is some great victory that will coerce reality.

The "ethics of tolerance" is also strange in that no one actually believes its message. Imagine someone so odd as to really believe that all human demands were equally worthy, that taking pleasure in sadism (even with a willing victim) is as worthy as taking pleasure in Mozart, that female circumcision is as worthy as charity. Presumably they do not believe this. They merely hate ranking human demands so strongly that "not ranking" takes precedence over trying to alleviate suffering (by abolishing female circumcision). Well, if that is what you truly believe, this kind of ethics will make sense to you. But make sure that is what you truly believe.

Do not think that the absence of objectivity in ethics plus logic coerces you into such a belief. The mindless offspring of the tolerance school fallacy is parroting the phrase "don't be judgmental" at everyone who has moral principles. If you have any moral principles, you have to be judgmental. And you have every right to be.

The One-Way Street

The best evidence that those who pretend to accept an ethic of indiscriminate tolerance do not really do so is that they do not stand by it with logical consistency. It is fashionable to forbid moral criticism across cultural lines. In New Zealand, there are those who refuse to criticize Maori (the indigenous Polynesian population) for sexism, such as the practice of forbidding women to speak at important meetings. But if we really believe that it is wrong to deliver a moral indictment across cultural lines, Maori should be told that they cannot accuse Europeans of injustice.

The rule against cross-cultural value judgments has some common-sense validity. Sometimes, a pattern of behavior is malleable in our society, but if it were altered in a pre-industrial society, the change would virtually unravel the whole cultural fabric, and that may be too great a price to pay. But we cannot exempt people from criticism of their cultural practices at whim.

The tolerance school fallacy is really a version of the naturalistic fallacy. Let us rephrase the naturalistic fallacy to read: there is no logical bridge connecting propositions that that do not endorse certain acts as moral, with propositions that do endorse certain acts as moral. To assert the absence of objectivity in ethics has nothing to do with favoring some acts over others. It does not even favor some ethical propositions over others. It says all ethical propositions are in the same boat, no matter what acts they endorse. It says that no ethical proposition is worthy of regard except from those who internalize it. You cannot reason from this to the conclusion that I ought to refrain from interfering with (or condemning) anyone else's behavior.

Indignation and Ignorance

Most intellectuals do not really know what is at stake in the debate about ethical objectivity. Rather, they have a vague awareness that it is fallacious to argue from fact to values, and that this has led to the rejection of the notion that humane ideals are privileged. When they talk about "ethical relativism," they identify it with either nihilism or a mindless tolerance of all values or both. Editorial writers rail against ethical relativism as if it were as a matter of choice, and castigate people as wicked as if they choose to be "relativists." Either you have a case for the objectivity of your ideals or you do not. It is a mater of rationality not choice. And if you do not, the consequences are not so dire. These editorials exemplify the theme of this book: their authors are all university graduates. It would have been so easy for their universities to give them a little sophistication so they could think clearly.

5

But that is Unnatural – Words Best Never Said

Anti-Key: (5) Appeals to nature. *Of all the mistakes that plague moral argument, this one probably does the most harm. It has been used to cloud almost every issue from gay rights, to heart transplants, to the merits of butter, to property rights, to protection of the environment.*

Preview: *Being in accord with nature; non-interference with nature; imitation of nature; using "nature" sensibly; the limitations of philosophy.*

Appeals to nature are bankrupt in moral argument, but we cannot simply condemn them as examples of the naturalistic fallacy. John Stuart Mill (1806–1873) granted this in his great essay *On Nature*, from which some of the following is taken. It would be uncharitable to assume when a person says, "the test of good and evil is whether something is in accord with nature," that they are stating a logical identity between the word "good" and the word "nature." That would be merely boring. It would simply mean replacing one word in sentences with another, like a penchant for replacing "automobile" with "horseless carriage" wherever we found it.

Rather, they mean that "in accord with nature" is a test or criterion of whether something is good: that nature has a kind of goodness about it that makes it an excellent source of moral advice. If something is natural, that counts in favor of its goodness; if something is unnatural, that counts against it. My criticisms of this notion will focus on how it is used today. Plato and Aristotle have a different concept of nature, that is, as a template of what each thing really is that could provide information about its perfect

How to Improve Your Mind: Twenty Keys to Unlock the Modern World,
First Edition. James R. Flynn.
© 2012 John Wiley & Sons, Ltd. Published 2012 by John Wiley & Sons, Ltd.

state. I also think that they were mistaken, but that can be shown only by an in-depth analysis. Remember that throughout, we will be asking not whether we appreciate the beauty of trees and streams but whether nature can provide a criterion that tells us what is good and evil.

The Criterion of Being in Accord with Nature

What do we mean when we say that an act is in accord with nature? We can hardly mean the totality of nature and all of its physical laws. That would lead to the absurdity that everything we do is good. Every human act obeys the law of gravity, whether we throw a child off a roof or send a rocket to the moon. Every human act obeys the laws of chemistry, whether we poison someone or give hungry people food.

We can of course mean that the act is one that people are strongly inclined to do, such as have sex or love their children, or one that the majority of people are inclined to do, such as have sex with the opposite sex or tell jokes. But we must not commit the naturalistic fallacy: no fact about what things people are inclined to do implies that those things are right. Human beings are naturally inclined to be filthy, as attested to by how hard it is to teach children habits of cleanliness ("cleanliness is next to Godliness"). Most of us are inclined to flee danger, which is why we put our soldiers through basic training and get them used to the sound of live ammunition flying overhead. But filthiness and cowardice are not virtues.

Here, I will strike a persistent theme. When we say that cleanliness or courage or straight sex are "natural," we may mean that not acting on them threatens us with disease, or defeat in war, or collapse of the institution of the family. Some of these claims may be false (see Box 5.1), but at least they have some substance. However, note that when we say things like this, the word "natural" has disappeared completely and has been replaced by pointing to consequences human beings find evil quite independently of any reference to nature.

The Criterion of Non-Interference with Nature

If our concept of nature is the physical universe untouched by man, and we take this literally, it leads to the absurdity that everything we do is wrong. Every time I breathe, I change the composition of the air near me. This may

> ## Box 5.1   The institution of marriage
>
> As if the chief threat to the family were not perfectly straight people leaving their families as soon as they think they can find more pleasure elsewhere. Happily, there are still some couples that are truly committed. Vladimir Nabokov (of *Lolita* fame) was devoted to his wife Vera, and she to him. She protected him from people (he called himself a "social cripple") and attended every lecture he gave. Any student who whispered to another while her husband spoke was admonished: "Do you not realize you are in the presence of a genius?"

seem pedestrian, but it suggests something of great importance: we never imitate or protect all of nature but actually pick and choose. The unreflective do this unconsciously, that is, they single out certain acts as outraging nature without making explicit any reason for their choice, for example, that heart transplants are unnatural, while other heart surgery is not. This is largely a matter of what "interferences" with nature they have got used to and which are new. It took some time to get used to air travel: if God had meant us to fly, he would have given us wings (see Box 5.2).

Sometimes, it is conceded that everything we do interferes with nature, but what interferes less is recommended over what interferes more, for example, TV ads tell us that butter has fewer chemical additives than margarine. This is so silly (would anyone prefer water to wine because we do less to it) that it seems uncharitable to think anyone believes it, but they must or the ads would stop. It may well make sense to prefer butter to margarine because recent evidence suggests that is may be, after all, better for your heart. But once again, the word "natural" has disappeared, and something more informative, "better for your health," has replaced it.

The Criterion of Imitating Nature

This criterion immediately raises the question of what part of nature we should imitate. If we were to imitate the whole of nature, as Mill said, we would commit crimes worse than the Borgias (substitute Hitler). Nature kills the innocent with earthquakes, forest fires, tigers that carry off children in India. Unless we want to be very wicked, we have to pick and choose in imitating nature.

Box 5.2   God and lightning rods

Those who single out parts of nature as indicative of the intentions of God are worthy of attention. As Bertrand Russell (1950) relates, when an earthquake struck Boston, many New England divines pointed out that Boston had more lightning rods than any other New England city. Its inhabitants had tried to interfere with God's natural means of punishing the wicked (being struck by lightning). But God was not at a loss: he used an earthquake instead.

We will speak about the notion that there are divine purposes in nature in Chapter 15. But Russell gives us reason to be wary. He imagines God and the angels in a moment of boredom deciding to play creation. The universe is created and organizes itself into galaxies; some of these contain planets capable of sustaining life; long-chain carbon compounds become self-replicating; life evolves into people; they build cities and fight wars, at which point, God erases the whole thing and says, "Well, that was an interesting game, we will have to play it again sometime."

The example of heart transplants being labeled unnatural is not invented. A columnist in my local newspaper branded them as such. She asked how God, at the time of the resurrection of our bodies, was to decide who gets the heart, the donor, or the recipient? She did, however, find some solace: after reading an account that pigs' hearts might be used, she cited this as welcome evidence against evolution. At least apes' hearts had not proved suitable. Such people are irreplaceable. I enjoyed her letters to the editor. At a time of unemployment, she remarked that people had not complained during the great depression of the 1930s: they had merely drunk blood from the veins of household pets and got about their business.

If we are humane, we point to benevolent processes in nature, things like the fact that most species care for their offspring. If we are anarchists, we point to things like the fact that there is no private property in nature that makes something mine rather than thine. If we are vicious, we point to natural selection as the survival of the fittest, with the implication that human beings should engage in cutthroat competition, rather as if observing the fact that the planets have circular orbits means that we should run about in circles. In every case, we do not borrow from nature impartially but rather use our pre-existing moral principles to judge nature, which means we already had them and did not get them from nature.

The Criterion of Preserving Nature

This immediately raises the question of what part of nature we want to preserve. I wish everyone wanted to preserve parks from real-estate developers, mountains from strip mining, the diversity of species alive on earth, and so forth. But the point is that these are things that many of us value, and that is the only reason they are valuable. Unless you believe in ethical objectivity, nature has no intrinsic value.

Often, viewing nature, the moon shining on the surface of the ocean, or the wonderful complexity of an ant colony, or the magnificence of a polar bear, arouses such a sense of the sublime that we feel that nature just must have some intrinsic value. The best way to dispel this notion is to emphasize, once again, that we pick and choose. The disappearance of the Arctic ice would be bad for polar bears but favor other species that could enlarge their habitat. The disappearance of whales would be nice for the sea creatures they eat. The preservation of a lawn means killing weeds (plants we do not enjoy as much as grass).

It is one thing to believe that "nature" has some property that renders it intrinsically valuable. But believing that all of the multitudinous parts of nature each have a varying amount of this property, varying amounts that rank them in a nice hierarchy that just happens to correspond to our degree of admiration, is another. Nature has value to the degree we value it. When you kill fleas for the benefit of your dog, you make a choice that nothing in nature tells you how to make. I think people are deficient if they take no pleasure in areas that do not show the visible hand of man. But there is no short cut to persuading people to have a better-developed aesthetic sense. To tell them that their posture is unnatural makes no more sense than to tell gays that their sexual practices are unnatural.

To defend the preservation of nature on the grounds that we want a habitat on earth that allows human beings to survive is, of course, the old story of substituting a word for "natural" that makes more sense: self-preservation. In sum: the use of the word "natural" in moral debate is always counterproductive. When it means anything, it is far more informative to replace it with a word that refers to the valuable thing implied (health, self-preservation). Its real use is as a bullying word. Telling you that something is "unnatural" is to play a trump card that wins the debate. You are supposed to slink away defeated.

Using "Nature" Sensibly

The fact that you should not use natural/unnatural in moral debate does not mean you should be so pedantic as to purge "natural" from your vocabulary, when it has a use that does no harm. It would be awkward to grope for another word every time you say something like, "It is only natural to care more about your own children than your neighbor's." We all know what you mean: that love makes people who are near and dear to us special. You are not using "natural" to rig a debate in your favor.

The Limitations of Philosophy

What you have learned from philosophy may prove ineffective when you actually debate with other people. The motives people have for not being open to the truth are legion. They may feel so threatened by the truth that they simply will not heed evidence. Religious people who believed that the earth was flat founded Zion, Illinois. When someone took their leader up in an airplane so he could see the curvature of the earth, he contended that the earth merely looked round from that perspective. If a person abandons reason, reason is powerless, but that is nothing new: you cannot convince a stone that the world is round either.

That does not mean you should give up. When Martin Luther King went to Montgomery, Alabama, most whites were impervious to evidence that blacks were not permanent children. However, when they saw that blacks had the self-control to boycott the buses, the intelligence to operate a complex car pool, the courage to accept violence without retaliation, some whites began to change their minds. They said to one another, "I am not sure I could undergo all of that for what I believe." Highly visible evidence that stereotypes are misleading can be more effective than rational argument.

Whatever the limits on our ability to persuade the non-rational, the debate that counts most is the one you conduct inside your own mind. If you learn how to use logic and evidence to examine your own principles, and the principles other people urge upon you, you can enlist in the ranks of mature moral agents rather than in the army of stones.

Reference

Russell, B. (1950) *Unpopular Essays*, George Allen & Unwin, London.

Part 2
The Truth about People

6

Random Sample – Quality Not Size

Key Concept: (6) Random sample. *Whenever a politician, or anyone else, does not like the results of an opinion poll, they ridicule it by pointing to the fact that only 400 people, or even only 1000 people, were polled. It is time for this to stop.*

Preview: *Quality not size; statistical significance; why people prefer bad polls.*

A little social science helps you understand everything from public opinion polls, to IQ and its significance, to the race and IQ debate; and it allows you to evaluate studies that presume to inform you about medicines, special education, how to teach mathematics, contraception, and what surprises the future has in store for us. I will begin with a question one hears every time an opinion poll is published: "Why should I trust a poll of only a few people, if I want to know how 130 million Americans intend to vote?"

Quality Not Size

The answer is that if you get a truly random sample you do not need huge numbers, and if you get a biased sample, huge numbers are of no help. A random sample is one in which every member of the population being polled has an equal chance of being included in the sample. Selecting by chance accomplishes this, and any other method introduces a bias.

Indeed, the greatest virtue of a random sample is that it is not a biased sample. In 1936, Roosevelt ran for re-election for President against Landon,

How to Improve Your Mind: Twenty Keys to Unlock the Modern World,
First Edition. James R. Flynn.
© 2012 John Wiley & Sons, Ltd. Published 2012 by John Wiley & Sons, Ltd.

and the Literary Digest conducted a huge telephone poll that predicted he would lose. He won by a landslide, and the Literary Digest went out of business. In those days, during the Great Depression, many working class Americans had no phones, so the sample was biased toward the well-off; the well-off were conservative, and many hated Roosevelt. You can now see why numbers cannot save a biased sample. If your sample excludes most of the 50 million Americans who are poor, you can poll all of the remaining 250 million Americans and do nothing to remove the bias.

Statistical Significance

Aside from being free of bias, the wonderful thing about a random sample is that we can use mathematics to calculate the numbers we need to get reasonable accuracy. The results may surprise you. The population sampled may be as large as you like: it could be 300 billion, and that would make no difference. If you can get a random sample, you simply do not need very large numbers.

Assume you have a jar with an infinite number of balls in it and that each ball represents a voter. Also, assume that the true split between Democrats and Republicans is even, so half of the balls have a "D" on them for Democrat, and half have an "R" on them for Republican. To get a random sample, every ball in the jar must have an equal chance of being selected every time you pick one out. That is not difficult. If you pick a ball without looking, put it back each time, shake the jar well each time, and do 400 picks, you will have a random sample of 400.

Most people want at least 19 chances in 20 that they are correct. Actually, I am not sure that is true of people in general, but it must be true of social scientists. If you have ever heard someone say that the results of a study are "statistically significant," that means the odds that something is true are at least 19 out of 20. Let us call the range within which your chances of being right are at least that good the "confidence limits."

The larger the sample, the smaller the confidence limits. Sticking to 19 chances in 20 that you will be correct, a random sample of 400 will give ± 5% as confidence limits. In other words, if your sample puts the Democrats at 53%, the chances are good that the Democrats are somewhere between 48 and 58%. That is too close to call. But with a sample of 1000, the confidence limits are down to ± 3%, and with 10 000 it is ± 1%. Box 6.1 provides a simplified formula for the accuracy of random samples of various sizes. It also provides a "proof" that random samples need not be huge.

Box 6.1   Accuracy of random samples

The formula (for an accuracy of 19 chances out of 20) is to take the square root of the sample size; and divide that into 100. Examples:

The square root of 400 is 20; 100 divided by 20 is 5; confidence limits are ± 5%.

The square root of 1000 is 32; 100 divided by 32 is 3; confidence limits ± 3%.

The square root of 10 000 is 100; 100 divided by 100 is 1; confidence limits ± 1%.

Imagine picking balls out of a jar evenly divided between those marked D or R.

Sample size = 2. There are only four possible samples, and all are equally probable: *RR DD* DR RD. So, two balls might just as easily put the Democrats at either 0% or 100% rather than at 50%. The confidence limits are huge: ± 50%. Our chances of being off by that amount are also 50%!

Sample size = 4. There are 16 possible samples, all equally probable:

DDDD	DDDR	DDRR	DRRR	*RRRR*	RRRD	RRDD	RRRD
RDRD	DRDR	RDDR	DRRD	RDRR	DRDD	RRDR	DDRD

You now have only two chances in 16 of putting the Democrats at either 0% or 100%, and you also have only a 12.5% (2 / 16 = 0.125) chance of putting the Democrats off by more than ± 25%. Just raising your sample from 2 to 4 has brought a big improvement.

If you want one chance in 20 of exceeding your confidence limits, a sample of 4 is useless, of course. Use the formula. The square root of 4 is 2; 100 / 2 = 50, so the range of error is ± 50%. The above just gives you the "flavor" of the proof.

When predicting an actual election, pollsters want something better than how voters intend to vote at one point in time, say three months before the election. They want to track trends that state who is gaining or losing as the campaign progresses. So, they usually take samples of 400 week by week and then a larger sample, perhaps 1000, right at the end. They can only approximate a random sample. The expense of getting a list of 300 million Americans, picking 1000, and running them down would be too much. They get what is called a stratified sample. They select widely dispersed districts that have been typical of past elections and, when they get their samples, weight them to make sure they are representative by gender, class, and so forth. They allow for people they have missed. Even today, a phone poll will omit the very poorest.

Why Some Prefer Bad Polls

The rare occasions when the polls predict the wrong result in an election are always celebrated as proof that polls are unreliable. Usually, the polls are wrong because the election is too close to call and/or because many people made up their minds how to vote only during the last few days of the campaign. Some voters make up their minds only when actually in the polling booth on Election Day.

The fact that the pollsters are usually right shows how good their sampling really is. The message is this: approximating a random sample is far more reliable than biased samples, no matter how large the latter may be. When someone derides a properly selected poll because the numbers are relatively small, or recommends a large poll with a clear bias, they may be ignorant. More often, they like the result that a bad poll gives and therefore prefer it to a good one. The bad polls they like are usually ones where self-selection intrudes, such as people having to phone in or mail back a preference.

Our City Council proposed to spend millions to build a new stadium and wanted to show that there was majority support. Therefore, they mailed ballots to every household: sports fans could be counted on to send back their ballot, while many elderly and poor people would be unlikely to respond. The poll gave the desired result. Then, an academic conducted a proper poll based on a random sample and interviews. The results showed that the stadium had only minority support. It was ignored. TV programs rarely care about the accuracy of their polls and just invite their viewers to phone in. This introduces two kinds of self-selection bias, who happens to watch the program plus who happens to phone in their preference, but it makes for exciting TV.

Taking Bad Polls Without Realizing It

The criteria for a reliable poll are relevant to everyday life. People are apt to judge character after a few encounters, even to fall in love at first sight. If you take the total range of behavior of a human being as your population, a small sample of how someone behaved on 10 occasions is hardly adequate. If it is courting behavior, it is also a biased sample. Every politician tries to get you to judge him or her from a few samples of behavior on television. We tend to internalize powerful stereotypes of people we do not know at all, from Tony Blair, to Diana, Princess of Wales, to Mother Teresa. Behavior on TV or even behavior as friend, spouse, boss, student, these are not unbiased samples. Whenever you form an opinion about someone, ask yourself about the quality of the sample.

7

Intelligence Quotient – Hanging the Intellectually Disabled

Key Concept: **(7) IQ (what it means).** *The fact that IQ tests are sometimes used inappropriately, or the fact that they register racial differences, has made them suspect, particularly in America. This is no more sensible than discarding tape measures because sometimes people make mistakes when they use them, or because they show that some children are shorter than others.*

Preview: *Understanding IQ scores; adjusting IQ scores; death row; significance of IQ scores.*

The first step toward understanding what IQ scores are all about is to understand that they are based on norms. That means the scores are based on how a random sample of the population did when they took the IQ test For example, if you are an American, and your performance exactly matches that of the average American of your age, you get by definition an IQ of 100.

Test publishers go to great lengths to select a normative (or standardization) sample that approximates as closely as possible a random sample of the population. Like the pollsters, they select a stratified sample rather than literally a random sample. They select schools scattered throughout the whole nation and then discard some until what remains is typical of the nation in terms of urban/rural, rich/poor, black/white, and so forth. They come very close to randomness. Recently, I analyzed 14 combinations of IQ tests and found that their samples of American schoolchildren were accurate to ±0.75 IQ points. Their samples for adults were accurate to ±1.50 IQ points. A good estimate for Wechsler and Stanford–Binet

How to Improve Your Mind: Twenty Keys to Unlock the Modern World,
First Edition. James R. Flynn.
© 2012 John Wiley & Sons, Ltd. Published 2012 by John Wiley & Sons, Ltd.

tests in America, the best going, is that their norms are accurate within one IQ point. That does not mean that your IQ score is to be trusted, as we will see.

Understanding IQ Scores

What is an IQ score? It is a comparison of the number of items you get correct with the performance of a sample of your age group presumed to be representative. If you are 12 and get exactly the average number right for your age group, you have by definition an IQ of 100. If you score above average, let us say better than 84% of your peers, you will be assigned an IQ of 115. The technical reason for this is that the 84th percentile equates to one standard deviation above average, and the value of an SD is set at 15 points. If you look at Figure 7.1, you will see the famous normal curve. The numbers immediately below it refer to the number of SDs an IQ score is above or below average. But you will be mainly interested in what your IQ means in terms of percentiles.

As Figure 7.1 shows, an IQ of 145 means that you are very nearly above 999 people in a thousand. A score of 130 puts you above almost 98% of your peers. Someone at 85 has outperformed only 16% of their peers, and

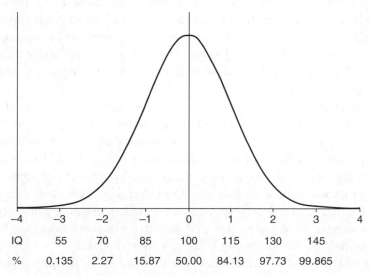

	−4	−3	−2	−1	0	1	2	3	4
IQ		55	70	85	100	115	130	145	
%		0.135	2.27	15.87	50.00	84.13	97.73	99.865	

Figure 7.1 Standard deviations, IQ scores, and percentiles.

someone at 70 only about 2%. A score of 70 is usually used as the cutting line for intellectual disability. To get a really accurate estimate of your IQ, it would be best that you be tested every other year from 8 to 16, because on any given day you might have hay fever or be upset, the examiner might make an error, and so forth. Also, you might switch to a better school, join a new peer group, or do something that challenged you more and promoted your cognitive development.

Adjusting IQ Scores

I have documented an interesting trend, namely, the "Flynn effect" or the phenomenon of massive IQ gains over time. This means we cannot take IQ scores at face value. Remember that IQ scores convey a message: where you rank against your peers. That means against people of the same age. No six-year-old can be expected to match the performance of a 12-year-old, and no 70-year-old can be expected to match the performance of a 35-year-old (unless they are superior for their age).

You must also be compared against people of the same age *at the same time*. That is because even people who suffer from intellectual disability would rise on the percentile scale if you compared them with people of the past. Common sense tells us that someone with a score of 70 on today's norms could be average if compared to people of the same age from the Stone Age. In fact, overwhelming evidence tells us that an American at 70 on today's norms has equaled the average score of people of the same age in 1916. The average American has gained 30 IQ points over the century, at least on Wechsler and Stanford–Binet tests, and this appears to be true at all levels of the IQ scale.

There is an interesting issue here. Someone might argue that twentieth-century IQ gains should be taken at face value as intelligence gains. However, this proposition has a number of implications that make it improbable. Take people with an IQ of 40 on current norms: they would have had 70 against the norms of 100 years ago. After all, 30 points gained since then means they would have all done 30 points better when compared with people from that distant time. If the gains are simply intelligence gains, people with a score of 40 on today's norms should strike today's clinical psychologists as mentally competent, and this is far from the case.

No matter what we decide about the significance of IQ gains, your IQ score has to be adjusted downward if you take an IQ test with obsolete norms. Your IQ score is meant to tell you about your percentile rank compared to your peers. If you are 17, what point is there in knowing what your IQ would have been if you had been 17 some 20 years ago? You compete against the 17-year-old of today when you go to university, and therefore, you want to know how you rank against them. IQ gains in most English-speaking nations have proceeded at a steady rate of 0.30 points per year on the mainstream IQ tests. To adjust your IQ, do the following. First, find out what test you took and what year it was published. Assume it was the WISC-III (Wechsler Intelligence Scale for Children, Third Edition) published in 1991. The sample was selected and tested two years earlier, which takes us back to 1989. If you took it in 2009, your IQ has been inflated by 20 years of obsolescence. Therefore, your IQ has been inflated by 6 IQ points: 20 years × 0.30 points per years = 6. If you got an IQ of 126, adjust it down to 120.

Death Row

Lowering your IQ may hurt your vanity but for convicted murderers, it may save their lives. In America, people cannot be executed if they are not mentally competent.

To show that they are not mentally competent, you must produce IQ scores 70 or below from tests taken at school. Take identical twins convicted of a capital offense. In 1975, as children aged 11, one takes the WISC-R (Wechsler Intelligence Scale for Children, Revised Edition) whose norms were relatively current at that time. The standardization sample was tested in 1972, so there is only a three-year lag between him at age 11 and the 11-year-olds who normed the test. He gets an IQ of 67 and lives. In 1975, his twin happens to attend a different school. There, he takes the old WISC whose norms had not been updated since 1947–1948 (when its standardization sample was tested). So, now there is a 27.5-year lag between him at age 11 and the 11-year-olds who normed the test. Thanks to being compared to 11-year-olds from the distant past, when average performance on the test was worse, he gets an IQ of 74.35 and dies. But the extra points have nothing to do with his mental competence – it is entirely the work of the obsolete norms!

Do we really want to make life and death some kind of lottery? To make death depend on whether a school psychologist had been prompt in buying the latest version of the WISC, or whether because of a limited budget decided to use up copies of an older version, is unacceptable. I have conducted a campaign to get courts to adjust the inflated IQ scores of those on death row. This has not been easy, because every prosecuting attorney and every psychologist they hire as an "expert" tries to confuse the court about what IQ scores mean. No prosecutor or prosecution expert has had the courage to admit that they are getting people executed who simply had bad luck as to what IQ test they took as a child.

The Significance of IQ Scores

I have written a book, *What is Intelligence?* (Flynn, 2007/2009), arguing that the debate about whether IQ tests measure intelligence sheds little light.

It is better to focus on what they tell us about a person's conceptual skills and knowledge, and what implication they have for his or her ambitions. A combination of high-school grades and Scholastic Aptitude Test (SAT) scores has a correlation with university grades of about 0.40. The SAT is really a hybrid that merges an IQ test with measures of academic achievement. For now, assume that a correlation of 0.40 is high enough that elite universities are likely to use it to screen prospective students. So, your IQ score tells you something about whether you are likely to qualify for a good university. It tells you less about how you are likely to do if you get in. Motivation and self-discipline are at least as important as IQ. With the same qualification, IQ scores also tell us who is likely to qualify for a wide range of jobs, and even things like how well they avoid accidents and illness in everyday life.

The fact that IQ scores tell us something significant when we compare individuals within groups has led to comparisons between groups and between nations. Here, I must at least hint at what I believe IQ gains over time mean. I believe that they signal gains in the kind of cognitive skills needed in a scientific and technologically developed society. Some groups, such as black Americans, may be less integrated into that society and thus do worse on IQ tests without reflection on their innate capacities. Over the last generation, black Americans have gained more than 5 IQ points on white Americans, but they are still about 10 points behind white Americans.

People in many developing nations are just beginning to modernize, and IQ gains among them are really beginning to take off. Certain of their cognitive skills (those relevant to reasoning about abstractions) lag at present, but they are very likely to catch up with the developed world over the next century. Those who tell you that developing nations lack the intelligence to create a modern industrial society go beyond the evidence. The average IQs in developing countries today are at least as high as ours were 100 years ago, and we have certainly developed such a society.

Reference

Flynn, J.R. (2007) *What is Intelligence? Beyond the Flynn Effect*, Cambridge University Press. (Expanded paperback edition 2009).

8

Intelligence Quotient – and the Black/White IQ Gap

Key Concept: (7) IQ (and regression to the mean). *There is a correlation between IQ scores and life outcomes, such as how well students do at university or what professional qualifications they are likely to get. A correlation is a measure of regression to the mean. This concept has been used to suggest that blacks have inferior genes for IQ as compared to whites.*

Preview: *Correlations and regression to the mean; uses and abuses of regression; regression and race; regression not a cause.*

Sometimes, we do not want a random sample, but rather a sample of those who are above (or below) average for a certain trait. Assume we use a tape measure and select the 38 tallest people in a class of 100. If the height distribution approximates a normal curve (it usually does), they will average one standard deviation above the mean. One of the reasons we work with normal distributions, and measure where traits stand on them in SDs, is that it greatly simplifies the calculations. Take my word for this and the estimates that follow.

Correlations and Regression to the Mean

If you look back to Figure 7.1, you will see that our sample will average at the 84th percentile for height, because this is the percentile that corresponds to one SD above the mean. Height correlates with basketball-playing ability but not perfectly; other things such as reflexes and speed are important as

How to Improve Your Mind: Twenty Keys to Unlock the Modern World,
First Edition. James R. Flynn.

well. So, the correlation will be neither perfect nor non-existent but somewhere in between. Let us put it not at 1.00 or at zero but at 0.50.

A sample selected out for superior height and averaging at one SD above the mean for that will be 0.50 SD above the mean for basketball-playing ability. That is to say they have "regressed" half way to the mean. If the correlation had been perfect, they would not have regressed at all, but would be one SD above average for basketball as they are for height. If the correlation were nil, they would regress all the way to the mean, signaling that height is no predictor at all of basketball-playing ability. Sir Francis Galton (1822–1911), a half-cousin of Charles Darwin, discovered correlations and the concept of regression.

It was immediately realized that these concepts gave useful information. Take our group selected to be one SD above the mean for height. One SD above the mean corresponds to the 84th percentile; 0.50 SD above the mean corresponds to the 69th percentile. Selecting on a trait correlated with basketball ability gives a group of pretty good basketball players.

It is now clear why elite universities besieged with applicants would use standardized tests to screen students. Recall that the correlation between the test scores and university grades was 0.40. If they admit those who average two SDs above the mean on the test (a score of 130), then 0.40×2 SDs tells us how far they will regress. They will be about 0.80 SD above average for university grades. This is the 79th percentile, so their entrance criteria gave them students who will average better than four-fifths of Americans, and allowed them to discard the rest. Figure 7.1 is not detailed enough to equate fractions of SDs to percentiles, but Google a table of areas under a normal curve, and you can do all the equating you like.

Uses and Abuses of Regression

There is a trap here. Before you can put correlations and regression to the mean to work, you need to not only have an elite group but *know how they were selected*. Imagine you just found a sample of students in a room and happened to measure them for height, and found they were one SD above the population mean. So, you think they will regress downward toward the mean for basketball, but then you find they were picked out as the best basketball players in the population! You would now say, well if the correlation is 0.50, they must have chosen a group that was two SDs above the mean as basketball players. Otherwise, they would not have regressed to where they are for height ($2\,SD \times 0.50 = 1\,SD$ of height). So, they are really at the 98th percentile for basketball – I'll bet this is the university team.

As this makes clear, regression to the mean applies not just when social scientists select a sample but to everyday life when society selects a sample. Universities select out the best basketball players to make up their teams. But anything that involves competition selects, and often the criterion that operates involves both excellences for a trait plus some good luck.

When rookies play their first season of baseball or cricket, batting averages select out an elite who did best, but over one season, luck affects performance. You may have happened to benefit from fielding lapses or pitchers/bowlers having an off-day. You cannot transfer good luck to the following season, so it is unlikely that the correlation between your performances between the two seasons will be perfect. As a group, the elite rookies are likely to regress toward the mean, and their batting averages will drop. Track and field is different. How fast you run the 400 m over a particular season, assuming no injuries from one season to another, owes almost nothing to luck. Any variation from one season to another will be due, not to one season being an elite sample of your performances, but to real-world factors, such as growing maturity or being past your prime.

Academic competition for grades in a particular course selects out an elite that gets an A+. But within some areas, the correlation between courses is far more perfect than within others. Within mathematics, the best student in differential equations is likely to be the best student in algebraic geometry and in number theory, and so forth. Within political studies, the best student in political behavior is less likely also to be the best student in areas as diverse as international relations, political philosophy, and quantitative methods. So, talented math students will come to scholarship committees with a string of A+s, and talented political studies students with a mix of A+s and As. Rather than putting all the math students at the top, the obvious thing would be to alternate science/math students with arts/social science students. Observe how quickly math professors forget what they know about regression to the mean when such a proposal is put.

In sum, when you know the trait on which an atypical sample was selected, you can use their score on that trait to predict their score on another: just allow for regression to the extent to which the correlation is imperfect. When you do not know the trait that was used to select, you may have a correlation and know all about regression to the mean, but you are helpless.

Another warning: you must be aware that a correlation between two factors does not tell you that they are causally related. There may be a third factor that was used for selection of which you are unaware. For example, scholars have studied America's black population and looked for a correlation for above-average IQ and above-average lightness of skin color. This idea is to discover whether blacks with the highest degree of white ancestry thereby have an IQ advantage. However, high-achieving black males prefer light-skinned black women. Since these men have better genes for IQ, the children of such a pair will tend to have both a higher IQ than average and a lighter skin than average. So, there will be a modest correlation between light skin and above-average IQ purely because of sexual selection.

In the general population, there is a correlation between IQ and the length of a woman's legs between hip and knee. Men prefer women with that kind of long legs, and in the competition for desirable women, men with high status (and above average IQs) tend to win. The daughters of such a pair will tend to have both attractive legs and higher-than-average IQs. Long legs do not cause higher intelligence; sexual preference forges the correlation. Note how discriminating men are: they do not just prefer long legs but prefer a particular kind of long legs. They have souls.

Regression and Race

You are now in a position to understand Arthur Jensen (born 1923) and the race and IQ debate better than most psychologists do. Jensen looked at studies of identical twins raised apart. He found that they were far more alike for IQ than were randomly selected people. Since they did not have family environment in common, this could only be because of their identical genes. The difference between the adult IQs of twin and co-twin was so small that the effect of family environment on IQ looked very feeble; indeed the correlation between the two was at most 0.33. Family environment is the kind of environment that is likely to separate black and white children, that is, black families are usually poorer than white families, the parents have fewer years of schooling, and so forth.

A gold star if you can anticipate Jensen's argument. Let us assume that blacks and whites are identical in terms of genes for IQ. Then, blacks can be treated as a sample of the general population selected out for poor environment. Since we know how they were selected, we can put correlations and regression to the mean to work. At the time Jensen wrote, blacks on average were one SD (or 15 points) below whites for IQ. Therefore, with a correlation of only 0.33, they must have been selected out as a group with an environment 3 SDs below the white average. After all, 3 SDs times 0.33 equals 1 SD of IQ deficit. Given regression to the mean, anything less than 3 SDs would not account for the 15-point deficit. Now, look back to Figure 7.1. If blacks were that far below whites for environment, the average black environment would have to be worse than that of 99.865% of whites. Who could believe such a thing? The average black would have to be like a drunk lying in an alley on skid row.

To rebut Jensen, you have to dig deep. The calculations are perfect. However, his argument has certain hidden assumptions, and Bill Dickens and I have made these explicit. His argument assumes that genes and environment do not causally interact as people age, omits dynamic factors of great potency that operate between groups, and (in my opinion) omits evidence that black subculture insulates blacks from the kind of cognitive challenge whites enjoy. This last will become plausible a few pages hence when you read about Elsie Moore. She found that white and black families, both impeccably middle class, were quite different in their child-rearing behavior, with large consequences for the IQ of their children.

Regression not a Cause

It is important to really understand regression to the mean. The most damaging confusion is to think of it as a real-world cause. I will give two examples.

The correlation between parental height and child height is not perfect. Therefore, if we select a sample of parents taller than the average, their children will tend to regress to the mean and be shorter than their parents. Similarly, if we select a sample of parents shorter than average, their children will tend to regress to the mean and be taller than their parents. Does this not mean that the present generation must be clustered more closely around the mean than the last generation? And that after a sufficient number of generations, we will all be the same height?

First, let us see why there is regression in the children of tall parents. During sexual reproduction, there is a random element in how the genes from one parent combine with those from the other. On average, those taller than most will have had better luck in the genetic lottery. No doubt, there are also environmental factors affecting height that are a matter of luck, perhaps ones having to do with nutrition while you were in the womb.

On average, those taller than most will have had better luck here as well. You cannot pass luck, whether better or worse than average, on to your children. The children of lucky parents will tend to have only average luck and therefore regress to the mean.

We now see that regression to the mean is an artifact of selecting out an atypical part of a generation, that is, it is an artifact of a certain kind of sampling. If we had selected out a random sample of a generation, that kind of sample would not show the average child either shorter or taller than the average parent, unless real-world causes were at work. Luck would even out: parents would on average have had typical luck for height, and their children would on average have typical luck.

Sampling artifacts are not actual causes that affect the real world. The last generation was not a sample drawn from the present generation. If the two generations differ, they have been differently affected by causes, just as if two oak trees differ. What might actually produce a new generation more clustered around the mean for height than the previous generation? There would have to be a real-world cause that reduced height differences. For example, if you shot all the people who were taller than average before they could reproduce, there would be less variation in the genes that affect height. Or if the mothers of the present generation gave their children a more uniform diet than their own generation had enjoyed, there would tend to be less height variance in the present generation.

The same analysis holds for IQ, of course. If we select a sample of high-IQ people, their children will tend to have IQs closer to the mean; if we select a sample of low-IQ people, their children will tend to have IQs closer to the mean. But unless something happens in the real world to lessen IQ variance (like more uniform nutrition), there will be no tendency for IQ differences between people to lessen with each generation.

Early in the debate over race and IQ, two scholars (Block and Dworkin, 1976) suffered from exactly this kind of confusion. They said the average black has an IQ 15 points below whites. But we all know that the correlation between IQ or measured intelligence and true intelligence is not perfect. Therefore, thanks to regression to the mean, we know that the true intelligence gap between blacks and whites must be less than 15 points. They remarked that they had never encountered this argument. One hopes not. Badly measured blacks are not a low-IQ sample of a population of perfectly measured blacks (or whites for that matter). There is no population of perfectly measured anybody.

If you use an imperfect instrument, the mistake can be in either direction. I measure my son's height and am later told that the yardstick is defective. Until I know how it was biased, I would not know whether it put him too tall or too short. Perhaps an analysis of IQ tests would show that they are accurate measures of white intelligence but underestimate the intelligence of blacks. However, you would need real-world evidence of that fact, not just talk about regression to the mean. Arthur Jensen had a field day. As he said, the Block and Dworkin argument consisted of page after page of statistical gibberish. This was not very polite, but it was true.

Reference

Block, N.J. and Dworkin, G. (eds) (1976) *The IQ Controversy: Critical Readings*, Pantheon, New York.

9

Control Group – How Studying People Changes Them

Key Concepts: (9) Placebo effect; (10) charisma effect; (11) control group. *Correlations cannot be taken at face value because of the interference of third factors. The concept of using a matched group to control for interference is simple, but in practice, it can be either difficult or impossible.*

Preview: *Hidden factors; sugar pills and the "hypnotic state"; doctors and pharmacists; control group; good luck, making your own luck, unavoidable bad luck.*

There is a correlation between ice cream sales and the incidence of hay fever, but eating ice cream does not cause hay fever. The warm weather and pollen of spring are the "hidden" causes of both. Recall some earlier examples. Blacks with higher IQs may tend to be light-skinned. However, the only reason that light skin is correlated with higher IQ may be because black males prefer to marry partners that have light skins, so sexual preference rather than white ancestry is the cause of the correlation. Women with longer legs (from hip to knee) may tend to have slightly higher IQs. However, this is only so because men prefer women with legs like that. In other words, when there is a correlation between two things, it may be not because one influences the other, but because a hidden factor causes the relationship.

Hidden Factors

The hidden factors are called confounding variables. Overlooking these may seem such an obvious mistake that no one would commit it. However, it is an ever-present danger because of ignorance. If you were not aware of

How to Improve Your Mind: Twenty Keys to Unlock the Modern World,
First Edition. James R. Flynn.
© 2012 John Wiley & Sons, Ltd. Published 2012 by John Wiley & Sons, Ltd.

the mating preferences of American blacks, how could you imagine it was lurking in the background? When told that children from homes where vocabulary was limited had small vocabularies, President Kennedy seized on this as the answer to underachievement at the start of school. It did not occur to him that parents with inferior genes for intelligence would not only speak to their children with a substandard vocabulary but also pass on their inferior genes. He was not alone in finding environmental explanations of individual differences welcome and genetic ones unwelcome. You will find journals full of articles that control for everything but genes, and whose findings are therefore worthless.

Other preferences also make people resistant to acknowledging confounding variables. A member of my family took a correspondence course from a teacher education department. She was given readings that emphasized that the use of corporal punishment was correlated with youth crime. When she noted that poverty might account both for the use of corporal punishment and for the frequency of crime, she was told that she would do well to rethink "her views in favor of corporal punishment." The lecturers were so committed to the notion that corporal punishment was the source of all evils, they simply could not acknowledge the possibility of a different underlying cause. When you find a correlation that pleases you, play devil's advocate and try to imagine every loathed confounding variable that could account for the results.

Sugar Pills and the "Hypnotic State"

Over time, scholars have collectively become aware of possible confounding variables that would be unlikely to occur to anyone on their own. Doctors discovered that when a patient was a given a sugar pill, but was led to believe it was a real medication, their condition improved, which shows how the mind influences physical health. This is called the "placebo effect." Some studies indicate that when psychoanalysis works, it is not so much because the analyst possesses a unique understanding of the human psyche (trained as a Freudian, Jungian, or Adlerian), but because people respond well to the notion that a competent professional knows what is wrong with them and wants to help them. They even improve after they get on a waiting list to see a psychiatrist.

The mind can also enhance physical strength. Australian male undergraduates were given a heavy object to hold at arm's length. Their performance improved amazingly when told that the average female under-graduate could do so for 5 min. They did feats thought possible only when people were in a "hypnotic state." It is unclear that there is anything that subjects do under hypnosis that cannot be duplicated with ordinary incentives.

Doctors and Pharmacists

The persona of the person who administers a treatment can be a factor in why something works. You may get better results from a drug your doctor recommends than when a pharmacist recommends the same drug.

This is called the "charisma effect," and it goes well beyond medicine. When innovators or their disciples, fired by zeal and self-belief, introduce a new method of teaching mathematics, good things can happen. They are often harder working, more competent, and more sympathetic than the average teacher, but in addition they are more impressive. They inspire respect or even awe among teachers and students who begin to believe they really can improve, and therefore approach mathematics in a new spirit. Usually, the new method stops working when handed over to the mass of teachers throughout the school system for whom it is merely another in a series of innovations, one similar to those they have been ordered to try over and over throughout their careers.

Control Group

Once you become aware of the danger that confounding variables can deceive you, you want to take steps to eliminate their interference. The usual way of doing this is to supplement the group of subjects you are studying with a second group, called a control group. Indeed, the first question you should ask when presented with a so-called result from a social science study is whether or not a control group was used.

It is relatively easy to control for placebo effects by way of a "blind trial." A large number of people are assigned randomly to two groups: one is given the new drug, and the others are given a sugar pill. For obvious reasons, no one who has contact with the subjects or analyzes the results should know which is which. For equally obvious reasons, most purveyors of alternative medicines do not subject their products to such rigorous tests. They simply bombard you with people who testify that their drug "worked." As we have seen, sometimes the charisma effect can be controlled just by comparing the effects of a drug administered by one kind of person with the effects that occur when it is administered by another kind of person. If it rarely works unless a doctor or psychiatrist administers it, and there is no chance that diagnosis plays a role, something is odd.

When controlling for a new teaching innovation, varying the personnel is difficult. Ideally, you would want both the new and the present method taught to randomly selected students by randomly selected teachers, but it is hard to avoid the teachers who are assigned to the new method hoping for better things and those assigned to the old expecting the same old results. Hiring actors to convey enthusiasm to the control classes is expensive, and actors are unlikely to know much mathematics.

Good Luck

Sometimes luck sends data your way in a context that automatically incorporates controls. Norway mass-produces a new way of teaching mathematics over a decade when Sweden does not. A good example of this occurred recently. Assume you want to test whether or not remaining in work past age 60 keeps people mentally alert and impedes the cognitive decline associated with old age. The obvious problem is that if you divide Americans into two groups, one whose members have retired at 60 and one whose members are still working, you do not know what is cause and effect. If people still in work after 60 are more mentally competent, is it because work is exercising their minds, or because people who are more alert are less likely to retire?

In 2007, a group of social scientists realized that they had been handed a controlled experiment on a platter. Males aged 50 to 54 and aged 60 to 64, respectively, had taken the same test of episodic memory (one of the first cognitive abilities to decline with age). They came from 12 nations that had a variety of laws about compulsory retirement, which mitigated the factor of individual choice. Cross-national differences as to how many people stayed in work as they aged were unlikely to have anything to do with cross-national differences as to whether they were alert enough to stay in work. The social scientists found that if the percentage of males in work dropped by 90% as men aged (Austria, France), there was a 15-point decline in episodic memory. If the percentage in work dropped by only 25% (US, Sweden), the decline was only 7%.

72

Making You Own Luck

Good luck of this sort is rare. Take intervention studies in which you give children from deprived backgrounds an enrichment program. Perhaps the most famous of these was the Milwaukee Project. In 1967, psychologists at the University of Wisconsin selected a depressed area in Milwaukee, which, although it contained only 2.5% of the city's population, yielded one-third of children classified as mentally retarded by the city's state schools. In that school system, the cutting line for mental retardation was an IQ of 75 or below.

The psychologists wished to see how much effect giving these children a better environment, one that afforded the advantages enjoyed by upper-class children, would have on their IQs. From infancy, the experimental children spent most of the day, five days a week, at learning centers staffed by trained paraprofessionals. They were given a comprehensive program designed to promote their cognitive, language, social, emotional, perceptual, and motor development. They were also given good food and medical and dental care. In an effort to upgrade the morale of the home, their mothers received vocational training and training in home-making and child-care skills. They were given IQ tests periodically beginning at the age of two. How could one determine what was working? Was it the enrichment program, upgrading the home, or taking so many IQ tests (something that would give the children test sophistication)? And how could one control for genes?

The psychologists selected a group of mothers from the area: all were black and had a mean IQ of less than 75. As children were born to these women at the local hospital, they were randomly assigned to an experimental and a control group, thus controlling for genes (the mother's IQ is the best predictor of a child's IQ). The experimental group got the benefits of the total program. The controls got nothing but the periodic IQ tests, thus controlling for test sophistication. The sibling group was the brothers and sisters of the experimental children, and they got the testing and the benefits of upgrading of the home. The contrast group was the siblings of the controls, who also got only the testing, but by comparing them to the siblings of the experimental group, one could tell whether there were any subtle benefits children enjoyed when their siblings experienced enrichment.

What an elegant design. The experimental group scored 30 IQ points above the control group until the program ended at age six, enough so that few were ever classified as mentally retarded. An endless wrangle ensued about the fact that their educational achievements were not as high as their

IQs would normally indicate, and the fact that they lost much of their IQ advantage as they aged, but the main objective of the study was realized.

Unavoidable Bad Luck

The Wisconsin psychologists had a piece of bad luck because they could not allow for what was unknown until 1984: American children in general were making massive IQ gains over time. They had used the appropriate IQ test for the children at each age: the Stanford–Binet at ages two to three; the Wechsler preschool test at ages four to five; and the Wechsler schoolchildren test from the age of six onwards. However, these tests had been normed in 1932, 1965, and 1948 respectively. As we saw when we looked at the fate of men on death row, taking a test with outdated norms inflates IQs. The experimental children were being compared not to contemporaries but to the lower-scoring children of anywhere from 20 to 40 years in the past. As you can imagine, this meant that their mean IQ was bobbing about in a way that had nothing to do with what was happening to them. For example, they showed a drop when they left the program to go into inner-city schools, but the drop was underestimated: they went from a test normed in 1965 to one normed in 1948, which gave them a bonus of about 5 IQ points.

This does not mean that the elegant design was useless. The scholars in question kept their eye on the difference between their experimental group and their control group as an index of what was happening: that gap was unaffected because both groups were taking the same test at the same age. However, the unwary were jubilant at how high the IQs of the children were (above 120 as infants). They were deceived by IQ gains over time acting as a confounding variable and inflating IQ scores.

10

The Sociologist's Fallacy – Ignoring the Real World

Key Concepts: (11) Sociologist's fallacy; (12) percentage or ratio. *It might seem that nothing would be simpler than matching groups for comparison. In fact, it often means that real-world differences go unnoticed.*

Preview: *Matching for SES; matching for profession; the easiest kind of matching; under-identified models; Marx and Popper; Marx and history; meritocracy and history; concepts plus arithmetic.*

As we have seen, when you do something to people, that often introduces a confounding variable. Similarly, when you manipulate data, you may create a confounding variable without realizing it. The most common examples are cases in which matching two groups for one thing creates a mismatch for something else. This can happen in any area of science but it is much more likely in social science because numerous factors interact in a complex way.

Matching for SES

Take a situation in which three factors are inter-related such as genes, environment, and IQ. When people hear about the black/white IQ debate, the first thing they usually say is "but surely when you adjust for class, the black IQ deficit disappears." In fact, most of the deficit remains, but put that aside for a moment. How would we adjust for class?

You select a criterion for class, perhaps something like socio-economic status (SES), which takes into account the status of various jobs (doctors

How to Improve Your Mind: Twenty Keys to Unlock the Modern World,
First Edition. James R. Flynn.
© 2012 John Wiley & Sons, Ltd. Published 2012 by John Wiley & Sons, Ltd.

rank higher than unskilled workers) and the level of household income. The simplest method of equating home environments for class seems to be just to equate black and white homes for SES, for example, to compare the IQs of the children of black doctors who make $100 000 per year with the children of white doctors who make $100 000 per year. Having eliminated the effects of unequal home environment, we can make a comparison that allows us to assess the impact of possible genetic differences. If no IQ gap remained, blacks and whites must have equivalent genes for IQ. However, this would be a false conclusion.

This is because there is not only a causal link between environment and IQ, but also a causal chain that runs from genes to IQ to environment. Assume that intelligence plays some role in the competition to attain a high SES (you have to be more intelligent than average to go to medical school) and that intelligence is influenced to some degree by genes (Einstein had better genes than the village idiot).

Now assume that a smaller percentage of the black population qualifies to be a doctor than the percentage of the white population. If only the top 5% of blacks qualify as doctors, their children will inherit highly elite genes within the black population. If fully 15% of whites qualify to be doctors, their children will inherit elite genes within the white population, but their genes will be substantially less elite. Therefore, even if the children of black and white doctors have the same IQs, the black children are on average more genetically advantaged. And the larger population of blacks must be somewhat inferior to whites for genetic quality for IQ.

You might think that if we compared the IQs of the children of non-professionals, the result would be biased in favor of whites. In fact, that comparison would also be biased in favor of blacks. Think for a moment. If we subtract from the white population a larger percentage of those with its best genes, and subtract from the black population a smaller percentage of those with its best genes, which race does the resulting comparison favor? We can see this clearly if we exaggerate the percentages. Imagine I was comparing the bottom half of whites with the bottom three-quarters of blacks. Clearly, the whites would be a significant genetic residue, and the blacks much less so.

Box 10.1 spells all this out graphically. Study it and you will see why all comparisons that equate the races for SES will favor blacks. They all select out blacks with a higher genetic quality within their population than the whites with whom they are being compared. Remember: children get not only their home environment from their parents but also their genes.

Box 10.1 The sociologist's fallacy

The sociologist's fallacy: assume that fewer blacks have a high SES than whites.

Whites	Blacks
	High SES (much better genes than average)
High SES (slightly better genes than average)	Low SES (slightly worse genes than average)
Low SES (much worse genes than average)	

(1) Take comparing the children of blacks with high SES and whites with a high SES. If intelligence plays a role in the competition to attain a high SES, and if intelligence is influenced to some degree by genes, and if only 25% of blacks have a high SES as compared to 75% of whites, then: the blacks who achieve a high SES will be more of a genetic elite within the black population than whites are within the white population. After all, a black had to beat most blacks, and a white had to beat only the worst whites. (2) Now, take equating the children of blacks with low SES and the children of whites with low SES. The black parents are the bulk of the black population. The white parents comprise a small residue consisting of the most unsuccessful.

Therefore, any equating of the races for SES will create a comparison between black and white children such that the blacks will have a genetic quality that the white children cannot match. All such comparison will overestimate the effects of equating children for home environment. Home environments may have been equated, but the genes inherited have not.

This does not mean we cannot attack the problem, but we need a good research design. In 1986, Elsie Moore compared two groups: 23 black infants adopted by white middle-class families and 23 black infants adopted by black middle-class families (Moore, 1986). The white and black adoptive mothers had the same number of years of schooling, that is, 16 years. When tested at ages seven to 10, the black-adopted black children had a mean IQ 13.5 points below the white-adopted black children. Moore observed interaction between mother and child while the latter was trying to perform a difficult cognitive task. White mothers tended to smile, joke, give positive encouragement, and applaud effort. Black mothers tended to frown, scowl, criticize ("you know that doesn't look right"), and express displeasure. Children were more likely to ask for help from white than from black mothers.

Moore's design avoids the problem of what genes the children were inheriting from the parents who were rearing them (none). It is unfortunate that the numbers are small. We cannot be sure that no random factor favored the genes of the black children adopted by white parents as opposed to those adopted by black parents. Nonetheless, what a pity this study has never been replicated. It suggests something worth knowing: even if we could equate black and white parents for SES without the complication of loading the genetic dice, it would not be a fair comparison because of a bias in favor of whites. On average, children enjoy a more cognitively rich environment in a white middle-class home than in a black middle-class home.

Matching Professions

Another example of the fallacy of simply "matching" socio-economic groups arose with the "meritocracy thesis." This posits that the IQ gap between the upper and lower classes is expanding over time. Some sociologists tested this by comparing the IQs of professionals today with the IQs of professionals some 30 years ago. They reasoned that if the mean IQ of professionals had not risen from one generation to the next, the meritocracy thesis was refuted.

There was much less excuse for this mistake because it does not involve the complication of the role of genes. The percentage of professionals in America today is much higher than it was a generation ago. So, of course they are less elite for IQ. If everyone became a doctor, their mean IQ would be by definition 100. The data presented do not falsify the meritocracy thesis; they just show that "doctor" refers to a group of people that have changed over time. The proper test would be to determine (as I have) whether the top third in occupational status today have a higher IQ than the top third in the last generation (they do not, or at least their children do not).

Just as a car today is not the same as a car 30 years ago, what it is to be a doctor evolves over time. Actually, sociologists are more likely to take social change into account than psychologists. Arthur Jensen gave this kind of fallacy the name "sociologist's fallacy" only because it deals with a sociological category (SES). As for who commits it, no social science is immune.

The Easiest Kind of Matching

We have looked at cases in which matching is difficult. But often, matching is easy and is not done because of failure to apply simple arithmetic. Using the concept of a percentage or ratio may seem obvious, but it is something that will make you superior to most of the journalists that appear on radio and TV. People are often hypnotized by the alarming or awful consequences of something and, therefore, do not measure their frequency against the frequency of alternative consequences.

An effective contraceptive pill causes some deaths, so we forget that ineffective contraception causes an even larger number of deaths per capita, thanks to the risks of abortion or childbirth. A poison drop kills a few trees, so we forget that a huge number of possums, which ring bark trees, are killed at the same time. A few people suffer neglect under a system of socialized medicine, so we forget the huge number of the uninsured who go without in America.

Ratios are usually expressed as percentages. If 90% of people are white, and 10% are black, the ratio of whites to blacks is 9 to 1. If a new contraceptive kills only 0.01% and saves 1.00% from death by abortion or childbirth, the ratio of lives saved is 100 to 1 in its favor. I will not belabor the point because with such a simple concept, the main reason it is ignored is not so much that people are ignorant as that they have an axe to grind. If you are against contraception entirely, any reason to reject it is good enough. If you yourself have excellent medical coverage but a child to support at university, any rationalization that spares you the obligation to pay taxes for the benefit of others will appeal.

Ratios have an extra bonus. Sometimes, you are told that the number of robberies in a neighborhood has doubled. Find out the percentages. If the percentage of homes robbed has doubled from 10% to 20% that is alarming. If it has doubled from 0.001% to 0.002%, worry about something else.

Under-Identified Models

Before we leave the sociologist's fallacy, we must see it as a symptom of the most fundamental mistake of social science: losing touch with the real world. The fact that two groups of people are called the same name, both called high-SES or both called doctor, obscures the fact that they have differences as well as similarities. Social science uses models to predict trends. But all too often, these ignore what would have to happen in the real world for the trend to actually occur. These are called "under-identified" models.

Marx and Popper

Whether or not Marx believed it, some of his followers believe the following: he had discovered universal laws of history that necessitate a uniform trend, namely, all industrial societies will evolve from capitalism to socialism to communism. Karl Popper called this "historicism." He pointed out that even universal laws do not dictate uniform trends. Indeed, universal laws usually dictate a variety of trends because of the fact that relevant conditions differ. Therefore, all models that claim to predict trends without stipulating all of the necessary conditions are under-identified.

Physics is a far more exact science than economics or history. Yet, even it does not discover laws that dictate uniform trends. The law of gravity is universal, but it does not dictate that all objects will go around the Sun in identical orbits. The orbit depends on the size of the object, its distance from the Sun, and how fast it is moving. A planet close to the Sun must move much faster than one farther away to avoid spiraling into the Sun. A planet, whose velocity is sufficient to counteract gravity, or slightly more, has an almost circular orbit like the Earth. A planet with a surplus of speed but not enough to escape the Sun and go off into space has an elliptical orbit like that of Mars. Comets have very elongated elliptical orbits and, like Haley's comet, come back only after many years. Some comets are going so fast that they come from outer space, whip around the Sun, and then go back into outer space never to be seen again (they have hyperbolic orbits).

The laws of evolution, like natural selection, produce different trends under different conditions. Mammals evolved from nocturnal reptiles that did not need color vision, and therefore, virtually all mammals are color blind. Primates were slowly selected to recover color vision because they live in trees, and need much better vision than dogs and cats that live on the ground. Since human beings are primates, they have color vision, but interestingly, a large percentage of people (like myself) are color blind in their dreams. Cave fish after many generations became blind because vision is of no use in eternal darkness, and natural selection did not weed out mutations harmful to sight. The prospects for Marxist historicism seem dim, but let us look at what Marx says. The summary is simplistic, but if you investigate further, the message will still be intact.

Marx and History

Marx believed that the factory system divided people into classes. The capitalist class owned the means of production, the factories, the mines, and the mills. Therefore, they could dictate who was hired to work them. The proletariat or working class had to sell their labor to the capitalists on whatever terms the market dictated. The worker that was hired would be the one who could survive working longest for least. Girls were preferred in New England's early textile industry because they could stay alive and work with less food than men. Automation is no answer because it just lengthens the day a worker can put in before they fall into the machinery from exhaustion. You can work longer running a steam shovel than you can with a pick and shovel. Clearly capitalism is going to immiserate the working class. They are many, and the capitalists are few. Sooner or later, the workers will develop a revolutionary psychology and rise up. They will overthrow the capitalist class and seize ownership of the means of production, and when the market has been abolished, all will produce goods for the needs of all.

Over the last 150 years, it has been apparent that certain conditions should have been stipulated. The human race must not be exterminated or reduced to primitive savagery by nuclear war. The earth must not run out of the resources needed to support human life or an industrial society. Workers must not develop their own class hierarchy in which hard hats (construction workers) fear or despise workers "beneath them" more than they do capitalists – and vote Republican. The market must not give most workers sufficient possessions, games, and circuses to keep them entertained. The wealthy and their intellectual cadre must not control a mass media in which they foreclose discussion of redistribution of wealth by labeling it "socialism."

A real history of the American working class means taking non-class historical forces into account, most of which were "reactionary" influences. Workers came from rural Europe to an alien society in which the Catholic Church was the only familiar transplanted institution. Many white workers felt threatened by black workers (and the Simian Celt) and Mexican immigrants, whom they saw as competitors for jobs and as people they could compare themselves to favorably, just so long as law or custom labeled them as "inferior."

Meritocracy and History

The meritocracy thesis also predicts a trend on the basis of an under-identified model. Imagine the liberal/left succeed in minimizing inequalities of environment and privilege: indeed as a thought experiment, imagine that these inequities were totally abolished. We can then state a model with three propositions: (1) with all environmental differences gone, all remaining talent differences would be due to variance between individuals in genetic quality; (2) with privilege gone, talent would make its way to the top unimpeded and inferiority sink to the bottom; (3) therefore, good genes for talent will become concentrated in the upper classes and bad genes in the lower classes.

In other words, egalitarianism tends to self-destruct. The nearer we approach its ideals, the more the children of the upper and lower classes will tend to inherit their parents' occupations and income according to merit. The upper classes will become a self-perpetuating genetic elite with all the good things in life. The lower classes will become a self-perpetuating genetic dump: an underclass with demoralized neighborhoods, vermin-infested housing, dysfunctional families, and schools.

What this model leaves unidentified is the dynamics necessary for its prophecies to come true. Imagine an annual school cross-country race. The results will rank everyone for running performance and running genes only if certain conditions are met. Everyone must be obsessed with winning the race and therefore, train and try to the utmost. Everyone must have equal opportunity, namely, the same quality coaching, diet, medical care, and physiotherapy services. The same kind of conditions holds for the competition for wealth and the status professions. It will rank for genes for talent only if all are obsessed by that competition, and all have a level playing field.

Now imagine what would have to happen to dramatically reduce environmental inequality and privilege. We would have to become much less status-conscious and money-obsessed. The upper and middle classes would have to endorse enormous transfer payments out of their own pockets into the pockets of the lower classes. This would mean a sea change in people's motivations. So long as they had sufficient possessions and security, they would neglect the competition for wealth in favor of a multitude of pursuits they consider more self-fulfilling.

As for the emergence of an underclass, that is nonsense. If a group with all of the disadvantages of a demoralized, ill-housed, ill-educated, etc., class began to emerge, its environment would have to be topped up so that its children would have a level playing field. That is to say, a decent life would have to be guaranteed to everyone irrespective of merit. What would that do to incentives? Many people of talent might want more than the not-unattractive minimum, but how many will care about shaking the last dollar out of the money tree? The higher we push the quality of environment all enjoy, the less attractive the prizes left for the winners.

Concepts Plus Arithmetic

I hope I have convinced you that you can understand social-science methodology with very little knowledge of mathematics. There are eight concepts that it is essential to grasp. However, not one among them asked you to do anything beyond elementary arithmetic. Without that, I fear that you are the legitimate prey of every bad social scientist.

Reference

Moore, E.G.J. (1986) Family socialization and the IQ test performance of traditionally and transracially adopted black children. *Developmental Psychology*, 22, 317–326.

Part 3
The Market and Its Church

11

Creating a Market – Not a Frankenstein

Key Concept: (13) Market (supply and demand). *The concept of a market is essentially the law of supply and demand. If there is an undersupply of something people want, its value is enhanced by competition among buyers. If there is an oversupply, its value drops because of competition among sellers.*

Preview: *Doing economics; the market and racial profiles; what is money; when does a market exist; selecting who can participate (free trade); selecting tradable goods, services, and information; prices, costs, income, and profits.*

I am going to introduce you to the basic concepts of economics by example, that is, by using them to draw my own conclusions about the virtues and limitations of the market. I have found that nothing turns off students more quickly than an analysis that seems to lead nowhere: every statement qualified by "now here is what the Marxists would say," and "here is what Milton Friedman would say," and "here is what a new-deal Liberal would say," and so forth. My purpose is not to coerce you into agreeing with me but to empower you. Once you have mastered the basic concepts, you can go on to read the literature and draw your own conclusions. You will no longer be a helpless bystander who feels excluded by ignorance.

The Market and Racial Profiles

The concept of a market as a tool of analysis has a wide range. It illuminates not only economics but also social science in general. That is because there are patterns of human behavior that approximate a market, and others in

How to Improve Your Mind: Twenty Keys to Unlock the Modern World,
First Edition. James R. Flynn.
© 2012 John Wiley & Sons, Ltd. Published 2012 by John Wiley & Sons, Ltd.

which the influence of the market is powerful but not easy to discern. The following case is selected from several developed at length in my *Where Have All the Liberals Gone?* (Flynn, 2008).

When whites use racial profiles to discriminate against blacks, it is easy to put all of your eggs in the wickedness basket. The following assumes only one market factor: that people take costs into account when making decisions, and that this includes the cost of information.

Take a woman who has been widowed, has rooms to let, and needs a good return from rent. Two people come to her door, a 25-year-old black American male and a 25-year-old Korean American female. She is hardly going to bear the expense of hiring a private detective to check them out as individuals. She knows that one black male in three is incarcerated at some time for committing a felony and that many of them deal in drugs. She knows that Korean females are overwhelmingly quiet, restrained, and prompt in payment. Why should she take a 33% chance of real trouble rather than opt for virtually a sure thing? In other words, absence of color prejudice does not mean that someone will be color-blind. A rational actor will use race as a cheap information-bearing trait.

A bank has more apparently sound white applicants for loans than it has money to lend. They know that black businesses on average have less managerial experience and that their failure rate is significantly higher. If the bank incurs the cost of checking out every black to see if they are exceptions to their group, it will be at a disadvantage to its competitors. As evidence that these rational considerations are not necessarily tied to racial bias: successful black-owned banks invest outside the black community more often than white-owned banks; black landlords as well as white landlords prefer white tenants.

Employers use race as a cheap signal of skill, motivation, and attitudes toward authority. In 2002, 5000 résumés were paired for quality, one under a white-sounding name (Emily or Greg) and the other under a black-sounding name (Lakisha or Jamal). They were sent to 1250 employers who had placed help-wanted ads. The white names received 50% more callbacks.

Police resources are always stretched, and they stop young black males in expensive cars for random drug searches, or on the assumption that the car has been stolen. This is far more efficient than stopping everybody. Being hassled by police is a frequent and unwelcome experience for black males. There is a web story of a black male who whistled Vivaldi whenever he saw the police. The hope was that this would alter the racial profile. The strength of these profiles is conveyed by one statistic. Since 1941, white police have shot 25 black police working undercover in New York City alone. When you see a black man in plain clothes threatening someone with a gun, you assume that he is the criminal. The odds are that he is. No white working undercover has ever been shot.

The point is not that the use of racial profiles is morally permissible. The point is that without a market analysis, you fail to see that you will have to do more than erode crude racial bias to eliminate them. You will have to change the social statistics that lie behind their use. If you cannot eliminate their use, the best you can do is give blacks compensation for what they are bound to suffer in the market. This is called affirmative action.

What is Money?

We now turn to market analysis in the traditional sense. As a preliminary, I want to answer a question that students often ask, namely, why does money have any value? They know that it is no longer backed by silver or gold, and after all, it is just pieces of paper. Why not just print enough to make everyone rich, or at least make your nation richer than any other? It is only recently that we could give a fully coherent answer. Although humankind had been using money for thousands of years, only toward the end of the twentieth century did a consensus emerge on how to manage the money supply, and this holds the key to the basis of its value.

Start with barter. You have a small airplane, run into someone with 10 sports cars, and both of you consider the swap a fair trade. You might wait a long time for that to happen. It is better to have a market using money that establishes an equivalent price for both. That means that people in general are willing to pay the same amount for them, probably because the costs of production plus a reasonable profit are the same. Now, you can sell your plane for 1 million dollars and immediately contact a car salesman who will sell you 10 sports cars for a million each. Money is useful because it makes exchanges easier. Our target is now clear: the right amount of money in circulation is the amount needed to facilitate all of the exchanges people want to make.

But how much money is that? We know that too much money is in circulation if prices start to rise, which we call inflation. That happens if the sum total of goods and services offered does not increase, but the supply of money does increase, so too much money is chasing too few goods. The best thing is to have a central bank that controls interest rates. If it raises interest rates, borrowing money becomes more expensive. As people pay off existing loans, fewer new loans result in a net loss of money in circulation, and as the supply of money contracts, prices fall.

There is general agreement that high inflation is undesirable. Uncontrolled inflation means that people are uncertain about the terms of transactions. I am building a house at a certain cost in terms of today's dollars but will sell it in a year for inflated dollars, and who knows how much they will be worth? So, why not manipulate interest rates so that inflation is zero? If you make a mistake, you will get deflation, which is just as bad. To run my business, I take out a loan in today's dollars and set my prices in today's dollars. Then, money becomes worth more and I am trapped: I have to pay off my debt using the dearer money and drop my prices precisely because there is less money chasing goods. I am likely to go bankrupt.

The best target is something like 1–3% inflation. You want prices to fluctuate with demand, and at this point psychological factors come into play. Say the demand for motorcars falls off. Workers are reluctant to see the dollar amount in their paychecks fall, and sellers are reluctant to cut the dollar amount of prices. But something like that has to happen if they still want to sell cars. So, you "trick" them through 3% inflation. The workers get the same number of dollars in their paychecks, the seller gets the same number of dollars when cars are sold, but those dollars are now worth only 97 cents each. The wage costs of producing autos and the price of autos have both fallen with reduced demand. But those who have had to adjust do not feel as bad as if these declines were transparent.

Mild inflation that is predictable, inflation you know is going to be kept between 1 and 3%, does no harm. When you take out a mortgage, you know that you are not going to have to pay the debt back in dollars worth more than the dollars you are borrowing. The bank will not lose because it takes the predictable rate of inflation into account in setting the interest on the loan.

So, now we know both what money is and what stands behind its value. It is something we create to lubricate or facilitate exchanges. Therefore, the amount created should match the number and quality of exchanges that take place in a nation's economy, which is to say that a big and vigorous economy can justify more money than a small economy. So, the quality of the economy is what underpins the value of the money. And if a nation tries to inflate its wealth beyond that which matches its economy, there is an automatic corrective. Its currency will be inflated, and the rest of the world will discount its value by the amount of inflation, so nothing is achieved except doubt about the probity of its financial managers. We also know why nations have central banks that set interest rates so they can hit an inflation target.

A beneficial byproduct of our new understanding of money is that economic debate is more rational. In 1900, William Jennings Brian could get away with urging "free coinage of silver" as a way of inflating the currency and helping the poor: "You shall not crucify (the working man) on a cross of gold." Today, we debate whether the central bank should set the inflation target at 2, 3, or 4%, and look for empirical evidence as to which target will best grow the economy and create jobs. That is a considerable improvement.

When Does a Market Exist?

The concept of a market would be useless unless there were something in the real world that the concept fits. Most human societies never developed a market economy. Those that have exhibit a system of behavior that functions as follows:

- The actors are all those buyers and sellers who influence the price of tradable items.
- They exchange items in the form of goods, services, and information.
- The law of supply and demand governs exchanges and establishes a price for every tradable item.
- Exchanges are made when both buyer and seller find them in their interests.

Selecting Who Can Participate: Free Trade?

No society allows people to decide simply that they will be participants in a market. For example, those who possess stolen goods participate at their peril, which is to say the law must define legal ownership (that you have the right to sell something) before a market can operate. Otherwise, those who are productive are undersold because it is usually cheaper to steal something or take it by force than to make or grow it. The fact that the world is divided into nations means that international trade is often restricted by tariffs that bar (or render artificially expensive) foreign goods. If the world were one big nation with complete mobility of people and uniform laws to protect the public good, there would be no justification for tariffs or restrictions on free trade.

In fact, without affectionate attachment to national or local culture, the world would be a poorer place. New Zealand is at a great distance from world markets, which adds to transportation costs. Assume that this makes New Zealand a non-competitive producer of everything but scenery and agricultural products (its climate and soil give it unique advantages). Then, just as certain areas of America see their population shift to more economically competitive areas, New Zealand might lose some two-thirds of its population.

At a certain point, love of locale erodes if a "landless class" cannot get work. When you protect non-competitive local manufacturing with tariffs (that add to the cost of imported goods), prices are higher, and you are effectively subsidizing manufacturing from the profits of agriculture and tourism. But this may keep your landless class in work rather than having to send them on "colonizing expeditions" abroad. Whether the preservation of national societies at the cost of world economic development is worth while is not a choice the "market" can make.

Tariffs are sometimes justified by the fact that the goods imported are made by sweated labor. The rebuttal is that however bad the conditions of the workers in question may be, the local people value them more than agricultural poverty, and to destroy the market for their goods is merely to force them into even greater misery.

On the other hand, the criticism that free trade means an incentive to reap the advantage of low costs of production by ignoring the environment is unanswerable. That is because it is true, particularly since the local environment may suffer less than the global environment. Granted that there is a tendency for nations to become less environmentally unfriendly as they go from being developing to developed nations; witness the better practices of the US compared to China. But it is also true that no level of development has as yet reached the point at which a nation's imprint on the environment is sustainable: the US is very rich, and it has not reached that point.

The only solution would be to bar participation in the market by those "criminal" producers who threaten the public good of the human race. The Kyoto accords, not accepted by the United States, are a feeble attempt to do this. The sheer impact of growing industrialization may well degrade the global environment to a point that will lead to a breakdown of civilized behavior and world order. To get industrializing nations like China, India, and Brazil to limit their growth and standards of living would entail nations like the US agreeing to "de-industrialize" and lower their standard of living. Agreement on targets for a sustainable consumption of the world's resources and a sustainable world standard of living is something no one wants to face.

A free market might bring this about automatically, but no one thinks it will be allowed to do so. If market forces hurt the powerful, they will use their military to obtain advantageous access to scarce raw materials and favorable terms of trade, and disastrous confrontations will occur. Some kind of consensus is the only alternative.

Selecting Tradable Goods, Services, and Information

Certain goods and services are often forbidden: selling human beings as slaves, hiring children for sexual exploitation, or taking out a contract to kill someone. Today, some question marketing guns, cigarettes, and certain species of animals. There is nothing in the concept of a market that decides whether these goods and services should be allowed: it is simply a matter of morality. Sometimes to forbid them incurs costs. In the nineteenth century, the ruling elite in Britain reached a consensus that the slave trade, which was highly profitable, was wrong. Large sums were spent to deploy the royal navy to suppress the slave trade, with no resulting economic benefit.

You could adopt a policy of buyer beware concerning all goods, that is, allow the sale of fake drugs that let people die or poison them, tainted meat or canned goods, cars that are unsafe, and houses that may collapse. The market would supposedly select out the brands you could trust, and fabricating those brands would be unlawful. Experience has shown that the market is quite inefficient in this, and lots of people die along the way. Therefore, we have pure food and drugs laws, houses are inspected as they are constructed, and so forth. There are also laws against false advertising, that is, making claims about products that the consumer can check only after what may be disastrous use. These sometime apply to protecting investors against securities whose risks have been understated. What happens when this is not done in some way, neither by public nor by private rating agencies, became apparent in the great economic crisis of 2008.

Others may imitate your goods once you market them or simply copy what you write, compose, or film. Allowing "imitations" on the market tends to make it counterproductive to invest large sums in research to develop new drugs, products, or techniques, and therefore, we have patents. Composers, artists, and writers will be poor unless you allow them the protection of copyright or give them a subsidized wage at least partially insulated from the market (e.g. give them a university post). Sometimes what benefits a concern is a kind of information that must be kept secrete and cannot be protected by patent. This often gets the protection of laws against industrial espionage (your competitors planting spies) and enforceable agreements, so that when your employees leave you, they will be in supervised employment. That means you have to approve the jobs they take for a period of years, so as to try to forbid them just going over to your competitors with what they know.

The concept of a market also does not forbid certain services like a protection racket. You pay me, and I will not injure you or destroy your premises or goods. Allowing these services to enter the market is so counterproductive of economic health (and human welfare) that they are forbidden. There are those who would have no public police force to protect you, but would have you compete to hire private detectives. In practice, this makes protection a function of the ability to pay and the so-called private police function like those who run protection rackets.

Prices, Costs, Income, and Profits

The law of supply and demand, at least in a money economy, establishes a price for every tradable item. This allows the "invisible hand" to work efficiently. Consumers can compare prices (so long as there are no hidden prices). Therefore, sellers will have to compete to market a product that is equal in quality to the product of their competitors at the lowest price that will give them a profit. Inefficient producers will be driven out of business because others can make a profit from lower prices when they cannot. If there is a demand for a better-quality product, producers will compete to satisfy it, and again the lowest viable price will result. Profit arises when total income exceeds total costs.

There are ways of driving down costs that have been deemed morally objectionable. For example, taking advantage of child labor and of the fact that the second earner in a household may find it acceptable to work at a lower wage than the first earner (the cost of two people living together is lower than someone living alone). If the market drives down the wages of second earners and part-time workers, many of these are women, and their wage rates will be lower than those of males. Sometimes, it is advantageous for the employer to lower the pay or conditions of workers to a level that arouses moral indignation. Four-year-old children sitting in the dark all day in mines, conditions that kill off your (replaceable) work force at an early age, and pay at the lowest level that will keep workers physically able to work (women and children require less food) are the stuff of history.

There is a persistent theme in the above. It is unimaginable in a civilized society to create a market without exercising moral judgment every step of the way. Moreover, once created, the market is not some kind of a Frankenstein to be allowed to treat human beings as it wills. We have every right to structure (which means regulate) the market on the basis of what human beings decide ought to be done to protect people from harm.

Reference

Flynn, J.R. (2008) *Where Have All the Liberals Gone? Race, Class, and Ideals in America*, Cambridge University Press, Cambridge.

12

Market Forces – How they Take their Revenge

Key Concept: (13) Market (regulation of). *Once you understand the concept of a market, you can perceive how attempts to manipulate the market to benefit people may have counterproductive consequences.*

Preview: *Rent controls; school vouchers; price controls (unions); a free good; tipping; regulating wages and supplementing incomes; regulating inheritance; making a public park.*

We have established that it is legitimate to regulate the market in principle, but that does not mean that every attempt to do so is sensible in practice. The market is not some inert mechanism. Indeed, we ignore market forces at our peril, as we shall now show with a few examples.

Rent Controls

The market will provide housing for all individuals and families that have any appreciable ability to pay. Those whose incomes are low or intermittent will get accommodations that are cheap and may be of low quality. They may be firetraps, difficult to heat, have asbestos in their walls, be overcrowded so that there is no privacy (children have no place to withdraw and do homework), and be infected by vermin that make children sick. For example, cockroaches cause allergies and carry on their bodies 32 bacterial-related diseases, 17 fungal-related diseases, three protozoa-related illnesses,

How to Improve Your Mind: Twenty Keys to Unlock the Modern World,
First Edition. James R. Flynn.
© 2012 John Wiley & Sons, Ltd. Published 2012 by John Wiley & Sons, Ltd.

and two viruses (most physicians think that most of these can be transmitted to humans, but there is no agreement on the mechanism).

Regulations to make landlords provide safe housing raise the rents of the minimum standard of housing available. If owners must provide fire escapes, that adds to their costs and is passed on as higher rents. This raises the question of restriction of choice. Should a Mexican male, newly arrived in the United States, not have the option of accepting fire risk in exchange for a lower rent, one that would allow him to save and bring his family to America somewhat sooner? Three remedies have been used to give the poor housing that is both safe and within their means.

Rent controls may work under unusual conditions, but they supply no general solution for people who cannot pay for decent housing. Assume a substantial portion of your population is poor and that market competition has set the levels of rents. To stipulate a maximum that lowers the rent owners can charge is counterproductive because it ignores market forces. If rents are set below the market price, they reduce the profit allowed on the owner's investment to the point that it is a bad investment. Investors will put their money elsewhere, there will be no expansion of the stock of low-cost rental housing, and if the city's population is expanding, there will simply be no place for the poor to live. Existing tenants will have to fight to get landlords to finance repairs and maintenance. The only way the landlord can enhance his profit is neglect, and while the property may deteriorate, the landlord will not be concerned because he has an unsalable asset.

Rent supplements avoid these problems. The market sets the price of rents, and while safety regulations raise the minimum rent, tenants on a limited income get a portion of their rent paid out of public funds. Rent supplements are clearly preferable to rent control and appeal to politicians because they need spend only a limited amount and need raise little additional revenue from taxation. However, at a certain point, you may find that in order to give the poor decent rental accommodation, the government is paying the lion's share of the rent. At that point, it makes sense for the state to build or buy a stock of state or public housing.

Since state housing is non-profit, it eliminates the profits of the private owner as a cost, and the state can directly provide maintenance rather than coercing landlords by expensive legal procedures. It need not be nasty if you can resist class pressure to crowd it into a small area in the worst part of the city. It need not be lawless if you have a resident police officer in every building. It can promote home ownership by allowing tenants to build up equity in the home if they pay more than the stipulated rent (usually 20% of one's income). It gives the lower one-third of income earners a real chance at home ownership, something no society has ever achieved through the private housing market.

State housing can also be used to ease mobility for workers who need to relocate to follow jobs. If you wish to move from New York to Arizona, you can transfer your equity in your home to a vacant and equivalent state house there. Whether you have to pay the cost of removal depends on whether shifts to that area would lower unemployment and save the government money.

Schools Vouchers

Schools vouchers are meant to give children assigned to bad public schools (state schools in Britain) the chance to go to private schools with a voucher in hand. The private schools would send the vouchers to the government, who would reimburse the school at their face value. As of 2011, the usual sum proposed is $2500, based on the cost of educating a child in the state-school system. The impact of vouchers on a mixed system of private and public schools is a complex question, but it is easy to assess its implications if public schools are abolished in favor of an all-private system.

First, take an all-voucher school. The pupils would get whatever level of education entrepreneurs can provide at $2500 and still make a reasonable profit. Whether this would be worse than the worst public school today would depend on what could be provided at the price. If you set minimum standards, it would be like introducing rent controls. If no one could provide that standard and make a competitive return on their investment, all schools would charge more than the voucher entitlement; or they would try to cheat on the minimum standard (just as landlords stuck with rent-controlled housing cheat on the building code and neglect repairs).

Second, if a private school cannot charge a premium for pupils that burden a school with extra costs, it would be in their interest to refuse them entry, unless of course they simply neglect them and do not pay the extra costs of educating them to a minimum standard. Presumably any sane voucher system would give the parents of blind or deaf or mentally retarded children extra vouchers. But what of children who suffer from milder handicaps like dyslexia, hyperactivity, or attention deficit, or simply come from a home that is well below average in encouraging pre-school cognitive development? Is the state to have a huge assessment apparatus that gives every child a voucher classification, with voucher amounts based on knowledge of what extra funds certain children require?

The alternative would be for the state to be educator of last resort and provide its own schools for those the market finds it unprofitable to educate. This would abolish the practice of mainstreaming children with disabilities and would produce a lower tier of schools for the underprivileged that would have a very low status. It is hard to see why they would be better than the worst of the present public schools.

Middle- and upper-class parents would be free to pay more for education than the parents who must depend on the voucher alone. As taxpayers, they would do well to vote to freeze or reduce the voucher amount in that while they get back vouchers for their own children, they are subsidizing the vouchers of others. Their children would be most advantaged the closer the voucher came to zero.

The obvious remedy would be to prohibit any parent from paying more to educate their children than the voucher amount. Many like myself would support the system if it truly meant equality of purchasing power for education, even without an extra benefit for the underprivileged. There is no doubt that the wealthy would make sure that the value of the voucher would be set at a gratifyingly high level, so that their children would get a decent education. I have never seen a voucher proposal with that kind of prohibition.

Regulating Prices in General

Direct regulation of the price of goods is rarely any more sensible than trying to regulate the price of housing through rents controls. There are arguable exceptions, for example, when World War II created a huge and sudden demand by the United States government for things like steel. The demand was to be met by domestic industry, and it could not do so without a time lag. Enormous economic dislocation would have occurred if the government had simply outbid all private buyers. A period during which the steel industry was put under government control, and its production commandeered and allocated, was necessary. Note that there were few producers and an atmosphere of patriotism, and therefore little chance of a black market in steel.

Usually, price controls create a tug of war between the set prices and the market that the market tends to win. Throughout history, the appeal of price controls to protect consumers has been ever present. Medieval governments fixed the maximum price of bread. Unless other steps are taken to control the supply of the commodity in question, a price ceiling will create a shortage. If people cannot make a profit from supplying flour to bakers (you make bread out of flour and water), they will turn to producing something that is profitable, and there will be little bread to buy. The only solution is to set a quota for bread production and use public money to make it worthwhile for producers to meet that quota. This can be very cumbersome if extended to a wide range of goods: you must set a quota for every subsidized good and calculate the right amount to make it worthwhile for producers to meet every quota. Any supplement that is too high will inflate the profits of the producer, and any that is too low will not avoid a shortage.

Usually, price controls are not accompanied by subsidies to producers. When a shortage results, the consumer starts paying prices that may be more onerous than whatever money savings they enjoy. They begin to compete with one another in terms of who is willing to spend the most time in order to make a purchase. When the United States set maximum prices for gasoline in 1973 and 1979, dealers sold gas on a first-come-first-served basis, and drivers had to wait in long lines.

This means that the true cost of gasoline was hidden. You might fill your tank for $4 less than you would have paid otherwise, but if you had to wait 30 min, and your time was worth $8 per hour, you only broke even and, in addition, suffered considerable annoyance. There were strong incentives to evade price controls. Some gasoline was held for friends, longtime customers, the politically well connected, and those who were willing to pay a little cash on the side. This last can lead to a black market in which the set price is ignored. On the black market, the price would be higher than it would be if it were not illegal. Sellers face the risk of detection and penalties, and this adds to their costs.

These consequences can be avoided by means similar to those we examined in housing; that is, you can use price supplements rather than price controls. You let the market set the price of bread. People who buy it get a receipt they can send to the government and get, say, a 50% refund. But it seems odd to single out bread, and to give everyone a refund whether they are poor or not. So, you give people below a certain income food stamps that allow them to buy whatever they want at market prices up to a certain amount. They may sell these on a black market, but at least you have enhanced the incomes of the poor.

Other things are often beyond the purchasing power of the poor, and rather than having stamps for everything (food, schools, health, transport, computers for their children, and so forth), you can make services like health and education a free good. That does not mean it comes at no cost, but its cost comes out of the taxes people pay, and these may be progressive so those who can afford it subsidize those who cannot.

A Free Good

When the government makes something a free good, the rationing imposed by the market (the ability to pay) must be replaced by something else, assuming the service is too expensive to be given to all who will want it at no direct cost to themselves. The two obvious alternatives are rationing by merit and by need. You must qualify for "free" tertiary education by doing well at secondary school and not flunking out. If you simply overload the universities with students whose education the taxpayer is unwilling to finance, the quality of education will fall. It is even worse to both finance the universities inadequately, and finance them on a per-student formula that encourages them to overload themselves. Yet this incentive system often prevails.

You qualify for "free" medical care by need. However, even if the medical system is well financed, there comes a point where treatments are so expensive, and so few benefit, that the state cannot bear the cost. Sometimes, flying the sufferer abroad can lower the price, and a public appeal may be launched to help the family pay. But rationing of some sort cannot be eliminated. The aim is to make need the basic criterion and reduce ability to pay to an absolute minimum.

The Strange Case of the Conventional Tip

Before we leave prices, I will try to solve the puzzle of the conventional tip. I will use the restaurant industry to illustrate how much psychology explains, and how little market forces explain unless they are supplemented by psychology.

In some nations, a tip (service charge) is automatically added to the bill, amounting to a certain percentage of the menu price of the meal. In the United States, the level is a matter of convention, but the convention sets an expectation that limits behavior. You may vary your tip to recognize quality of service, but you do so by tipping just above or below the percentage set by convention. In my lifetime, the percentage for average service rendered has risen. Once, it was 10% for average service, 5% for bad, and 15% for good. Then, the percentage for average service rose to 15. Now, it is about 20% for average service, with 10% an insult. New Zealand has no tipping (with rare exceptions).

It would be interesting to investigate what determines whether or not a country has the tipping system. I suspect that more than a desire to recognize the quality of service comes into play. Leaving a large tip allows us to display our wealth by tipping more than others can afford to do. However, I am more interested in why the conventional tip exists in some places and not in others, and what sets its level. Since restaurants are subject to market economics in all places, this difference cannot be explained by the law of supply and demand but signals a difference in psychology. Given a purely market analysis, while there is a minor advantage for employers, it is subtle and becomes evident only after the system is well established. The total remuneration of employees will be about the same under either system.

I suspect that the psychological factor is that New Zealand service workers have a greater sense of dignity than American service workers do, and find the implications of a tip demeaning. Some years after we came to New Zealand, our family embarked on our first trip back to visit America. When we arrived, and a railway porter helped us, I knew I was supposed to tip but found I had only 38 cents in my pocket. He shouted, "Oh, a cheapskate huh," and threw the baggage against a wall. When we got back to Wellington, a hotel employee helped me carry a lot of baggage up to our room. This seemed an unusually onerous service, so I offered a tip. He said. "Oh no, just use it to buy a treat for the kiddies." This sense of dignity may be the last remaining inheritance from New Zealand's egalitarian past.

The psychology of workers is a non-market factor with social ramifications. When Riesman, Glazer, and Denny wrote *The Loyal and Disloyal* (Riesman *et al.*, 1954), they found that some American service workers felt so demeaned by their customers that they had competitions spitting into the salad dressing. I predict that this would be less frequent in New Zealand (see Box 12.1).

From the consumer's point of view, a conventional tip is simply another way of partitioning the bill: rather than the cost of the meal all being under one heading, it is divided into two. As for employees, law may dictate that they get the tips, but their boss has already factored it into their wages.

Box 12.1   The furniture movers

It is easy to forget what that relatively classless New Zealand was like. James Michener (1947), in his *Tales of the South Pacific*, tells of an American shopper in New Zealand seeing an item in a window display. The owner told him it was out of stock, and he asked if he could buy the one in the window. The owner shouted, "Come here Fiona, it's the bloody Duke of Wellington." I once witnessed movers unloading the furniture of an upper-class Englishman who began to order them about peremptorily. They calmly set the furniture down in the driveway and drove off.

In 1970, a newly arrived colleague from England caught a cab at the airport and, at his destination, offered the driver a tip. The driver was genial but said, "I'm not your servant mate." Servility was not a tradable item. Even now, it is not uncommon for workers to identify more with their customers than with their boss. When buying sheets for our children, the woman waiting on us said, "You don't want our sheets, they are top of the line and expensive – go down the block, and you can get some for half the price." You get sentimental as you age.

That is, market competition sets a certain rate for their overall wage, and the employers make an allowance for tip income and deduct that from the employee's pay packet. So, the tip does nothing to raise the wages of restaurant workers.

Why has there been employer pressure to encourage tipping and raise the percentage? Partly, this is a diagnosis of consumer psychology. When people decide to eat out, particularly at an expensive restaurant, they want to indulge themselves and to obscure in their own mind the price they pay. "Forgetting" about the tip and focusing only on the menu price of the meals makes it easier. It puts them in a frame of mind amplified when tourists make purchases abroad at prices locals would not pay. Partly, they are less knowledgeable of what the seller would accept, partly they are less accustomed to haggling and may find it undignified, partly in a poor country they may sympathize with the seller, but there is also a holiday mood, a sense of "We are here to have a good time and not count the pennies."

Aside from melting consumer resistance, the conventional tip has one solid advantage for the restaurant owner. It means that much of what he pays his workers automatically rises and falls with the volume of his receipts. If your wage costs are fixed, and your trade falls off, either you may not show a profit for that period, or you have to lay off workers you know you will need later if things improve. If tipping equaled the full amount of what you pay your workers, your labor costs would be a perfect match for your receipts, the former always being 20% of the latter.

I once assumed that before I die, the compulsory tip would rise to 30%, 50%, who knows how high. But now we see there is a limit. Let us assume that setting tipping aside, labor costs are only 35% of total costs. If tips go above that, there is no advantage to the owner. And if they do, the price of eating out is merely becoming unnecessarily expensive. I do not know what percentage of total costs goes to wages in the restaurant industry, but if I did, I could predict the maximum percentage of the compulsory tip.

Regulating Wages and Supplementing Incomes

Minimum-wage laws raise the income of low-paid workers by setting legal minimums for hourly wages. Those opposed to the minimum wage argue that it tends to create unemployment among the unskilled or drives them into the black market, that is, into working for employers who clandestinely pay less than the law provides. There is no doubt that a minimum wage makes unskilled workers more expensive relative to other factors of production. Take employers who make a profit because they are free to pay low wages to unskilled workers. Higher wages mean that investment in labor-saving devices, not attractive until now, becomes a better investment. Studies show that if you double the minimum wage, you may decrease the demand for unskilled workers by 20%.

This argument ignores something directly relevant, namely, that those who get the minimum wage tend to be a fluid labor force. They are often paid an hourly rate as part-time workers or offered jobs only at peak times. In other words, they tend to drift from one job to another and in and out of employment. If they were perfectly fluid, the whole pool of unskilled labor would share the 20% cut in hours worked. And for the time they do work, they would each get double the present hourly rate. Clearly anyone would prefer to work 32 h per week at $2 an hour, rather than 40 h a week at $1 an hour. The increase in the minimum wage does not really mean 80% of unskilled workers being advantaged while 20% get no work at all.

The alternatives to the minimum wage all entail government expenditure of some sort, which makes them less politically palatable. The obvious alternative to helping the poor by way of a minimum wage is to pay individuals or families extra benefits. This raises the question of whether these should be targeted benefits for various categories (blind, ill, unemployed, solo-parent) or an untargeted benefit that raises the incomes of all to a certain amount using a "negative income tax." This means that if you submit a tax form showing that your job paid you $5000 dollars for the year, the government would give you another $5000 to get you to the set income of $10 000.

Assume you qualify for this by being in work. This raises the question of who is in work. Are you in work if you work for your uncle 40 h a week for one cent an hour? The problem is larger than that. Employers can factor the government top up into the wages they offer (as they do with tips). Rather than paying you $10 000 for a job, they can pay $8000 relying on the government to make up the shortfall. The employee will be worse off the first year because he or she must wait until the end of the tax year for the tip. But employers who pay $10 000 will be stuck with an extra $2000 in wages in every subsequent year. I predict that many jobs that pay $10 000 today will be advertised for less than that to shift some of the wage bill to the state.

The universal basic wage is different. It would give a set amount to everyone, whether they chose to work or not, whether they were rich or poor. If the amount is sufficient for a decent life, and one does not live in an egalitarian oil-rich sheikdom (there are none such), this tends to exhaust public revenue for all other purposes, including the police.

Trade-union bargaining for wages has the same effect on employment as the minimum wage. If every worker in every area were covered by wage agreements, these would not only set a minimum wage but also stipulate wage levels for many skilled workers. Once again, the employer will hire fewer workers than he would if wages were lower. If the jobs of his workers are protected, he will let his labor force decline by attrition. If only some workers have union contracts, the others will share none of the benefits, and the jobs lost will be a burden on them alone.

This shows the flaw of economic analysis without a political dimension. Unions are a progressive force politically, sometimes the only organized group that can be counted on to lobby for a higher minimum wage, more benefits for those in need, and a more progressive tax system. Of course, they have to advantage their members or they would not exist. Non-members who suffer might well gain more than they lose by the policies' trade-union support.

Regulating inheritance

This differs from what has gone before in that when people die, they are no longer actors in the market. How much of the capital they leave behind goes to their heirs, and how much goes to the government (as an inheritance tax) is a non-market decision. It must be made by considerations of justice and the common good. You may think it unjust that people cannot hand down all of their capital to their children, or you may think that if the children of the wealthy inherit a huge fortune they did nothing to earn, that puts them at an unjust advantage over the children of the poor. You may think it unjust to have large disparities of wealth in your society and that inheritance taxes, particularly if spent on social services, lessen inequality.

As for the common good, some argue that social services not earned by labor corrupt people because they give them something for nothing. They refer to welfare payments, unemployment benefits, rent supplements, and so forth. The best rebuttal is to point out that inheritances, particularly large inheritances, must also be corrupting because they are a perfect case of getting something for nothing. The common good, of course, includes larger economic consequences. You may believe that leaving large accumulations of capital in private hands means it will be invested more wisely than if it were invested by the government, or that large inheritance taxes undermine the incentives of people to work hard and save. The rebuttal is that people are more likely to be productive citizens if social services give them good health and education and take them out of hope-destroying poverty.

The important thing to note is that the law of supply and demand does not dictate policy and that whatever decisions are made rest on ethics and psychology.

Making a Public Park

We have seen that the market is potent, but I wish to stress that there are some things we value that the market would never provide. For example, the market would not provide a huge park like Central Park in Manhattan (the center of New York City). The land would afford a much greater return to a private owner if used for housing or commercial premises, a return far greater that what you could make even from a Disney Land. Note that amusement parks are never located on prime land, or at least never located on land that was at a premium when the park was built. Even if an amusement park were viable, an overwhelming proportion of New York's residents might prefer Central Park in its present form to having easier access to a Disney Land. Market forces would leave them with no choice. At present, if they prefer a windfall, they can vote in a mayor who will sell off 843 acres of prime land.

Opponents of government interference in the market say that setting aside scarce urban land makes land scarcer still, and thereby affects the price of land and housing. Why should people pay artificially higher rents and prices for housing because some city planner thinks they would benefit from a park? This betrays a state of mind that I will discuss later under the heading of "market worship."

Central Park contains several lakes and ponds, extensive walking tracks, two ice-skating rinks, a zoo, a conservatory garden, a wildlife sanctuary, a large area of natural woods, a reservoir with an encircling running track, and the outdoor Delacorte Theater which hosts the "Shakespeare in the Park" summer festivals. It also serves as an oasis for migrating birds. It attracts 25 million visitors annually who presumably make some contribution to the city's economy and tax revenues. The land area of Central Park is 0.02% of the New York Metropolitan Area. If it raises the price of land in New York, it would do so primarily by making it a more desirable place to live than other cities. Those who do not like to pay this extra premium may wish to relocate to Cincinnati.

Market forces would not actually maximize the value of how land is used in New York. A public amenity that gladdens all who live there adds more value than taking about $100 off the price of a half-million dollar home (using the concept of percentage, you will have calculated that 0.02% times $500 000 is only $100).

References

Michener, J.A. (1947) *Tales of the South Pacific*, Macmillan, New York.
Riesman, D., Glazer, N. and Denny, R. (1954) *The Loyal and Disloyal*, University of Chicago Press, Chicago.

13

Market Worship – No Ritual Sacrifices

Key Concept: (13) Market (attitudes toward). *The market poses a danger, namely, it inspires a worship that blinds us to the fact that it is simply a human invention for certain purposes; and therefore, subject to moral judgment just like any other system of human behavior.*

Preview: *The Tennessee valley; universities and cargo cults; the market and environmental disaster; the market and benevolence; objectifying the market; future of the market; the market and its church.*

Worshipping the market, like all forms of idolatry, enfeebles rationality. It takes the form of several delusions. We have already discussed one of these, namely, the delusion that the market can deliver all public goods. The example of Central Park shows that this is not so.

The Tennessee Valley

I think that the Tennessee Valley Authority provides another example, but that is more debatable. At least, now you have the tools to sample that debate. The Tennessee Valley Authority was a massive public project that tamed the floods of the Tennessee River by dams that produced power. It created recreational areas and turned the whole regional economy around toward relative prosperity. Private capital never undertook the project because the investments were much too high, and the returns too distant.

How to Improve Your Mind: Twenty Keys to Unlock the Modern World,
First Edition. James R. Flynn.
© 2012 John Wiley & Sons, Ltd. Published 2012 by John Wiley & Sons, Ltd.

However, an alternative would have been to allow the Tennessee Valley to become depopulated by migration to less risky and more prosperous areas.

The sufferings of displacement would have been considerable, and many (the elderly) would have been left behind to live in poverty. However, displacement would have created an extra source of cheap labor from those forced to move to Chicago or Detroit. On the other hand, there would be an extra cost in the transmission of the power in that it would all go to distant places. There would be few left in Tennessee Valley to use it.

Universities and Cargo Cults

Universities differ, and their heads (presidents or vice-chancellors) differ. In the seven universities at which I have lectured over the years, I have noticed a trend, reinforced by the perceptions of my colleagues. My experience does not extend to universities like Harvard whose heads must raise millions of dollars and may for all I know have a rare psychology for which a premium must be paid. They also have an eminent faculty that is not easily managed (witness the deposition of Larry Summers at Harvard). However, 80% of us teach in very different circumstances, and what I say may ring true for the majority of academics. For what follows, if the shoe fits, wear it.

The trend to which I refer is toward heads that exemplify an extreme form of market worship: the belief that imitating the market can confer the benefits the market itself confers. The problem is larger than the universities as many of those who work in a school or public hospital will know. I suspect that schoolteachers, doctors, nurses, conservation workers, and so forth have noticed similar trends: the inflated status of managers, the drift of power and resources to the center, the distortion of an institution's mission; this last despite the fact that mission statements of pompous content and absurd length become a cottage industry.

I will call the kind of market worship in question having a "managerial psychology." This does not mean that most people trained in management share it: many of them would be too sensible because this state of mind leads to bad management.

When the heads of universities mimic what they think are market principles, they frustrate both its academic purpose and efficient administration. Of crucial importance is whether the head finds the over-bureaucratization of the university normal. The university must of course live within its budget.

But what concerns me is the allocation of resources within the university: the academic departments and the administration do not compete for customers. It is a command economy with resources allocated from the top. Here, I must introduce a second trend, one towards a flow of power away from academics toward the center. Gone are the days when Deans were elected by academics from among their number and, if they wanted a second term, had to stand for re-election. Today, they are hired and fired by the center and do its bidding. Academics can defend their resources from one another, but I have never seen them force economies on the center. Therefore, there are neither market nor political restraints on the administration. This means that there is no check on the growth of bureaucracy except self-restraint.

No section of the university can be trusted to exercise that. This is because there is no functional limit to the good any sector of the university can do in its own terms. If the library had absolute power, there is no absolute limit on how much it should spend. Who has ever seen a perfect library with everything one could ask? Who has seen a department of history with an expert properly funded in every area that should be taught or researched? Neither would acquire anything that could not be defended on its merits, but the results would be grotesque: a university most of whose resources are sucked up by the library or History department, and the rest starved.

When a university investigates its bureaucracy, it may find some waste, but that is not the point. If the administration is free to do everything an ideal administration would do, it undermines the rest of the university. They should investigate the power structure that privileges the administration over the rest of the university.

If the administration has a managerial psychology, they will tend to mimic procedures found in the commercial world. No one objects to calculating the cost of the various activities of a university and outsourcing services where savings can be made, but to ask History to make up a budget that goes beyond its flexible costs and includes its fixed costs is mindless. The administration can price the cost of the Department's plant and the salaries of its present staff, and so forth. All too often, there is a pointless exchange of information from department to center based on information that the center has to provide. The department makes mistakes, the center corrects, and the department resubmits. There is one exception to costing: the time of academics is not costed. It is treated as a free good. Like any free good, consumers (the administration) feel they can draw on it endlessly, in this case without rationing based on the merit or utility of the request.

Understandably, government often uses student numbers as its criterion for funding universities. Managerial psychology finds it natural to apply the same criterion within the university, whether this undermines its academic purpose or not.

If too few students take classical Greek or Philosophy, those departments are not cost-effective and should be eliminated. Never mind that it is the students who are most worthy of respect, even if few, who want to read Plato in the original. The allocation of staff to departments in terms of student numbers is corrupting. Universities are supposed to protect the public from graduates that do not know enough and from waste of public money spent on those with no serious purpose. Yet administrations set higher pass rates as targets without quality control of the product. Who ever ran a market enterprise in that way? They can get away with it because the inadequacy of a history graduate is subtle and the perils of defective brakes evident.

A weapon for everyone working in an institution infected by market worship: mimicking something under the delusion that you will thereby accrue the benefits of the real thing has a name. It is called a "cargo cult," after tribes in stone-age New Guinea that build a facsimile of an air plane in the hope that this will attract the real thing with its valuable cargo. We have less excuse than they do. Believing that a market can supply all human goods is at one remove from reality. Believing that a pretend-market can pay market dividends is at two removes.

The Market and Environmental Disaster

We must distinguish between two theses: that the market uninfluenced by anything other than its own law of supply and demand can preserve us from environmental disaster; and that we should devise plans to transform market forces into allies in our efforts to save the environment.

The first is predicated on extending private property rights to all valuable commodities and thereby making them assets that will be conserved. For example, as oil gets scarcer, it will cost more, and not only will it be used less, but also the owners will realize they have an asset of long-range value. Therefore, they will ration it to last as long as possible, giving us a lead-time to develop alternative sources of energy. This is flawed because it posits an oil company run by people with an infinite life span. Most stockholders want to maximize profits during their own lifetime or at least that of their children, and will not postpone reaping the benefit of high profits now in favor of even higher profits in the distant future.

Market competition for a resource often dictates exploitation without regard for the future. In rural India, many farmers can now afford to sink artesian wells to access ground water. The result is that ground water may soon be exhausted, and much of rural India will become a desert. In fact, many wells, however deep, are already dry, and the rate of farmer suicide is alarming. But what are the farmers to do? If you refrain from drilling, that just means that you will not get your share of the water while it lasts and will starve sooner than your neighbors. This is exacerbated by the fact that the snowcaps in the Himalayas are disappearing, and it is their seasonal melt down that feeds India's rivers.

The Indian example shows the flaw of "make everything private property and all will be well" argument. It is not easy to see how this could be done with the water table. You could make me the owner of all the ground water in India, and I could sell permits to allow each buyer to drill a certain amount. If I want my heirs to inherit the business (a big if), would I not want to conserve ground water and ration it so it would never be depleted? Well, it depends on my other investments. I might want to get a high amount of capital quickly to invest elsewhere. Even if I do not, others might offer me a huge price to sell them the ground water because they want to turn it into ready capital. There are endless imponderables.

This may strike you as a local problem. In Brazil, farmers on the edge of starvation have every motive to destroy the Amazon rainforest and convert the land into pasture and farms. Brazil comprises half of the world's rainforests and holds 10% of the carbon stored in the world's ecosystems. At the current rate of destruction, 40% of it will be gone within 20 years. The impact on the world's climate of releasing that carbon may be grave. The Amazon's "local problem" is everyone's problem.

Industries themselves do not believe that the market will conserve resources without help. *The Forest Stewardship Council* (supported by the forestry industry) encourages consumers to use their spending power, not as self-interest would dictate, but in so far as they are motivated by altruism. They demand that retailers of furniture and so forth document that their products are derived from legal logging and properly managed forests, and label them as such, so environmentally minded consumers can buy them over cheaper products if they wish: a good thing, but its potency should not be exaggerated.

No one has devised a scheme to make the air or the waters of the ocean private property, which means that no private concern need count their degradation as a cost. If factory owners spend to keep from polluting the air, or if anyone spends to avoid harmful accumulations of chemicals in the ocean, they take on a cost that puts them at a disadvantage with their competitors. The market will do the job of preserving a resource essential to human well-being only if preserving it pays a cash dividend.

To fight air pollution, ranging from nitrous oxide to acid rain and greenhouse gases, there are cap-and-trade programs. A government or international body sets a limit on the amount of a pollutant that can be emitted. Companies are given a pollution allowance, and if they pollute less than that, they can sell credits to other companies who want to exceed their allowance. The system adds to the profits of those who pollute less and adds to the costs of those who pollute more. In theory, those that can reduce emissions most cheaply will do so, achieving the pollution reduction at the lowest possible cost to society. This system is often distorted by manipulation of the market for trading emission credits. They are bought and sold like any other asset, and their price can be affected by long-term bets about their value, which means that their price can fluctuate wildly. Firms that have to purchase them to meet short-term commitments to stay within their pollution allowance can find their price exorbitant and unpredictable

Trading in carbon credits is sometimes seen as a better approach than a direct carbon tax on producers of carbon-based fuels like coal. It is usually more politically acceptable to the producers, but the tax produces a more predictable effect in that market manipulation is not a factor.

The Market and Benevolence

One of the defining characteristics of a market is that exchanges are made when both buyer and seller find them in their interests. This has led to exoneration of all those involved in market transactions from moral censure. A moneylender's rates of interest may be very high, but unless he or she offered the best rates available, the borrowers would go elsewhere. If you drive all the moneylenders out of town, no one can get credit however much they need it. The argument is sound in terms of moral censure of the moneylender, but it does not show that the market is benevolent. It does not excuse tolerating a situation if all of the alternatives that people face are terrible, and if they can be alleviated.

The best bargain for many families in rural Wales in the late nineteenth century who were landless and had no capital was to work in the mines. This was preferable to their only other alternative, namely, starvation. In order to survive, it was often in their best interest to all go into the mine, the father to dig coal, the son aged seven to crawl through the mine pulling a coal cart where the space was too narrow for a horse, and the son aged four to perch all day on a niche cut in the wall opening and closing the ventilation traps.

In Turkey today, the best economic opportunity for some mothers is the rose trade. You pick a restaurant that caters to tourists and has a big picture window, stand outside, and send your child in to sell single roses. If tourists do not buy, they look through the window and see your child return to you and get beaten. Trade generally picks up. If no one bought roses, the trade would disappear, but one fears that the next step would be the mutilation of child beggars as in India. Blind beggars do better than sighted ones.

Levying taxes to spend on child welfare can be challenged. It is argued that the money would be better left in private hands, because this would benefit all children through higher growth rates; and therefore, you have simply chosen to benefit some children at the expense of others. This poses a terrible choice for developing nations. How to balance the trade-off between using scare government revenue for welfare and using it to provide infrastructure for growth (usable roads) has no easy answer. Affluent societies, like the European Social Democracies, have combined high rates of growth with high levels of welfare spending. They have decided that it is better to have no abject poverty among the present generation, even if this means less affluence in the future. Clearly this is a choice dictated by your moral point of view, and the market cannot tell you how to make it.

Personifying or Objectifying the Market

Whenever I have spoken of the market being unable to do this or that, I did not intend to personify it, as if it could act like a person rather than operate as an impersonal system. Rather, I meant to convey that it is a simply a system without the capacity to plan and assess.

That said, our analysis preaches two messages. First, when we interfere with the market, we are not dealing with some inert organism. We ignore how market forces affect the consequences of what we do at our peril; witness rent controls. And I hope that I have convinced you that "economic analysis" usually comes down to asking one question over and over:

How would actors motivated by profit and loss behave in this situation? Depending on the actor, this translates into a series of questions: Would they shift their capital elsewhere? How would they cut their costs? Would they cut production? Would they be tempted by a black market? Once you get in the habit of asking these questions, you are on your way to understanding.

Second, the existence and potency of market forces do not make the market into a "natural" entity. Its laws do not have the status of the law of gravity. As we saw in Chapter 5, even if the market were natural, that would in no way fortify its credentials. But the truth is that it is a human creation. It cannot tell us who qualifies as a market actor, what behavior is permissible in market competition, what counts as a legitimate good or service, when people should be protected from market forces, the conditions under which assets should be inherited, how a university should be run, how to preserve ourselves from environmental disaster, or how to be benevolent. These questions must be settled by appeals to moral principles and human psychology, and what works best.

Future of the Market

The rules of soccer create a sport that enhances pleasure by participation or attendance. When it becomes an obsession, it does harm. Fathers treat their children as having failed them by playing badly, whole communities are depressed or elated at their team's standing in the league table, editorials are written about whether decay of the national character is the cause of the national team's defeat, and so forth. We suddenly realize that something that has its place in the scheme of the good life (enjoying sport) has infected us with a psychology alien to the good life.

The market is a way of maximizing production and the efficient distribution of goods and services. It has done this task so well that it robs us of ethical autonomy. It invades the criteria we use to judge our people and our nation. Those who do not play well, those who cannot or will not offer services to others that others want to buy, are failed human beings. If our nation falls down the league table of productivity, our nation is a failure, and any right-thinking citizen would go elsewhere for a higher wage. If the next generation does not have "more" than we do, the human experiment has come to a halt. If we ever stop to question the endless expansion of productivity, we are told that it is the only way to avoid unemployment. This renders the circle complete: we cannot imagine a society in which all have dignity unless all participate in the market economy.

If we avoid environmental degradation by way of a pact in which affluent countries cut productivity, an unanticipated bonus may be that we will recover our moral autonomy. Being fully employed may have to be forbidden, national pride will attach to limiting productivity with equity, and the next generation may recover the knowledge that too many possessions are a distraction from living life to the full. In Howard Spring's novel, *Fame is the spur*, a 19th century trade unionist, enjoying a cup of tea and fish paste on toast, reflects how wonderful it would be if only all of his impoverished neighbors had the same. Sanity has not receded so far into the past as to be inaccessible. No one wants grinding poverty, but making the economic game the measure of man lays bare a spiritual poverty that does us no credit.

The Market and its Church

Whenever anyone tells you that the market is worthy of worship, remember this: captives for religious sacrifice could be a tradable item.

14

The Economic Collapse of 2008

Key Concept: (13) Market (assessments and bets). *Those who have begun market analysis will want to apply their knowledge to current events. For example, the economic crisis of 2008 to 2009 seems bewildering. But all you need to make sense of it is what you already have, understanding how a market works, plus two things: the law of assessment inflation and the concept of a bet.*

Preview: *The law of assessment inflation; the housing boom; multiplying risk into an asset; the rating agencies; why the insiders did not care.*

An AAA credit rating in the commercial world is an assessment. It is supposed to mean that what you are buying has a solid value and a very low risk. The trend that paved the way for the economic crisis in American was that ratings became inflated in the sense that AAA was awarded to assets that were unsound. I will state a general law of assessment inflation, spell out a simple example, and then proceed to the more complex example of assessing investments.

The Law of Assessment Inflation

Positive assessments will tend to drive out negative assessments. This is subject to two conditions: a political condition that has to do with the balance of power; and a psychological condition that has to do with the balance of incentives:

How to Improve Your Mind: Twenty Keys to Unlock the Modern World,
First Edition. James R. Flynn.
© 2012 John Wiley & Sons, Ltd. Published 2012 by John Wiley & Sons, Ltd.

- Political condition. Those affected by an assessment must have more power than those who make the assessment. Power does not always go with numbers. The clergy are few, but at one time, they had virtually a monopoly of power within the church. It was only when ordinary church members could hire or fire the pastor that their numbers began to count. The result: the assessment of who would go to hell was watered down to virtually zero.
- Psychological condition. The shift from negative to positive assessments must not be nullified by reinterpretation. Whether this occurs is contingent on a tug of war between the incentives of those who are interested parties. Some may be too ignorant to reinterpret.

The Law of Assessment Inflation and Grades

We can now understand grade inflation. Over the last 50 years, the A grade has been awarded much more liberally, even though students have not improved correspondingly. Inflated A grades have driven out As earned by unusual talent and mastery of material. Or to generalize, high grades have replaced low grades because two conditions were met. Students and their families have become more powerful than university lecturers. Those who had the incentive to reinterpret the meaning of watered down grades were vastly outnumbered by those who did not.

There is a restraint, of course, that I have not mentioned. If you just offer a degree with straight As on the Internet, you have destroyed your credibility. You would be like a self-declared counterfeiter. But if you are Harvard competing with Princeton, your students will like you more if you give more As, and your high reputation maintains your credibility ("Our students are so good, they almost all deserve As"). The parents who pay tens of thousands of dollars want a degree for their money and a good grade-point average as well. Within a university, where all lectures have the automatic credibility of their credentials, lecturers who give high grades tend to attract more students than those who give low ones.

Lesser universities encourage lenient grades because their income often depends on their number of students, and anyone with high standards who flunks people is a source of financial loss. He or she also hurts colleagues because their jobs are threatened if other departments have more students and are therefore better financed. We can now understand how universities issue mission statements that set the target of lower failure rates. This seems insane because any lecturer can reduce failures to zero just by passing everyone. But it makes economic sense.

Grades are like counterfeit money in the sense that you can just print them. But they are not like money in that they are not legal tender. Unlike money, people are not obligated to accept them when they are presented to purchase goods or services. Therefore, government need not step in and make privately printed grades illegal. High grades help you get better jobs but not by buying them. They send a message that you are worth hiring.

You might think that everyone would simply reinterpret grades. Mostly As from a good university used to mean, "Highly intelligent, learned a lot, can do creative work without guidance." Now, it means only "In the top half of the class (at least at Harvard), probably bright, literate, and not lazy." So long as everyone acknowledges the trend and does not take the new As at face value, the effects of the trend would be nullified. You would simply use A + to make the sort of distinction you used to make with A. This is where incentive systems become relevant.

Those who have the incentive to reinterpret are mainly employers. For example, I suddenly realized that high grades no longer meant much when people who applied for university lectureships all had straight As. Therefore, I introduced supplementary criteria to identify who was really outstanding. I started asking applicants for the best thing they felt they had ever written and read it for originality. References were largely useless because the same forces that had inflated grades had inflated them. I would not take them seriously unless I knew the referee and could phone and say "now you are a friend, are you sticking me with a mediocrity?" It is sad to see the old boys network of "who you know" making a comeback.

Students and parents have no incentive to acknowledge how little high grades now mean; quite the contrary. Since they are popular, government not only does not forbid them but also plays games that depend on not looking at grades too closely. It knows that parents hate it when their child lacks basic literacy and numeracy, so we have the idiocy in America of "no child left behind" (no child left behind what?). Government cannot simply tell the schools to manufacture passes for everyone without giving the game away. So there are to be tests that "maintain standards."

Well, schools under intolerable pressure to make everyone numerate and literate will pretend they have, just as everyone cooked the books in

Stalin's Russia to show they had met their production quota. You make the tests ones that can be passed by rote memorization and spend school time having students memorize the answers to the tests. Or you cheat. During 2011, teachers were caught manufacturing passing exams in several major cities, although the worst case was Atlanta.

In sum, grades are a currency that can be highly inflated and still buy self-esteem and good will without affecting anything else, except indirectly of course. They extract the indirect price of self-deception about the altered messages they convey. But the deluded pay the price without knowing it, and the cynical are amused by the folly of it all. Sadly, government legislation based on delusion extracts a more concrete price. It orients the schools in a way no one would really want: teaching for test passing, dishonesty, and concentration on the marginal student at the expense of others.

Some academics realize that grades are messages and resent the fact that grades have lost their power to discriminate. Their very awareness meant they had to surrender to the trend. If I give a B when everyone else gives an A, I have done my students the injustice of sending a message likely to be misunderstood to their disadvantage. Everyone will think they fall short of even that not very demanding level of quality signaled by an A today. I have no right to speak a private language about my students that no one else comprehends.

The Law of Assessment Inflation and Securities

Assessment lay at the root of the 2008 economic crisis. What was being assessed were securities that were a mix of mortgage and credit card debt that was transformed and multiplied and multiplied. At each stage, the risk of building on such a foundation was ignored. These securities got a triple A rating. This is to say the law of assessment inflation bit, which means that its political and psychological preconditions held (more on this in a moment). All investment is a kind of bet, and when you bet, you want an assessment that reassures you that it is likely to pay off. Inflated ratings allowed banks and investors to enter a fantasy world in which they thought they were sitting on a mountain of gold when in fact, the gold was paper, and its value rested on a bad bet everyone was making together. The bet was on the continuance of the housing boom. When the bet was lost, it brought down the whole structure.

The Housing Boom

Figure 14.1 shows the extraordinary boom in house prices that occurred in America between 1997 and 2007. The gains in that brief period are almost five times those of any previous boom in American history (those of 1895, the 1970s, and the 1980s). Clearly, something unprecedented was at work. A prosperous decade is always likely to mean some rise in housing prices, banks have more money to lend, there are more credit-worthy purchasers, and even if they are not particularly credit worthy, they are unlikely to be unable to make their payments. The very fact of the boom insures this. It makes it sensible for a bank to offer even subprime mortgages (mortgages to those with low incomes) and do so even on payment schedules that the owner may be unable to meet. After all, the owner has an asset that is rising in value, so when the time comes that payments are difficult, you just refinance the mortgage on better terms and the payments will continue.

The graph in Figure 14.1 is accurate when it shows that the housing boom of 1997 to 2007 was unprecedented. It may look odd to someone who bought and sold a home for a profit during the period when it is relatively flat. This is because your profit may have come from improved location. Perhaps your house became more desirable because the city expanded to make you fairly central. But your selling price will have been averaged in with houses sold in less desirable locations (out in the sticks) to produce a flat trend overall. Also, remember that you must deduct inflation from your profit.

This scenario ignored a dangerous trend. By 2007, according to the National Association of Realtors, 21% of all home purchases were by investors. This is probably an underestimate because investors deceive banks. You vacate a home to rent it, then buy another home as owner-occupied, vacate it, buy another, and so forth. An investor may have 10 homes all on the bank's records as owner-occupied (you only finance one home per bank, of course). A housing boom always brings in speculators who buy or build housing and hope to make a profit on selling or renting, and a record housing boom brings in a record number of speculators. Mortgages that require no down payment maximize the numbers.

The greater the influx of investors, the more likely that the supply of housing outruns the demand for housing, though this was disguised for a while by the very fact that banks were so lenient in issuing mortgages. At that point, speculators find that they are having trouble selling and must

121

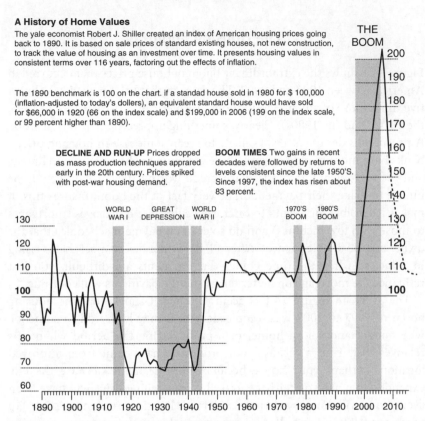

A History of Home Values

The yale economist Robert J. Shiller created an index of American housing prices going back to 1890. It is based on sale prices of standard existing houses, not new construction, to track the value of housing as an investment over time. It presents housing values in consistent terms over 116 years, factoring out the effects of inflation.

The 1890 benchmark is 100 on the chart. if a standad house sold in 1980 for $ 100,000 (inflation-adjusted to today's dollers), an equivalent standard house would have sold for $66,000 in 1920 (66 on the index scale) and $199,000 in 2006 (199 on the index scale, or 99 percent higher than 1890).

DECLINE AND RUN-UP Prices dropped as mass production techniques apprared early in the 20th century. Prices spiked with post-war housing demand.

BOOM TIMES Two gains in recent decades were followed by returns to levels consistent since the late 1950'S. Since 1997, the index has risen about 83 percent.

THE BOOM

WORLD WAR I　GREAT DEPRESSION　WORLD WAR II　1970'S BOOM　1980'S BOOM

1890 1900 1910 1920 1930 1940 1950 1960 1970 1980 1990 2000 2010

Figure 14.1 The property boom. Source: *Irrational Exuberance*, 2nd edn, 2006, Robert J. Shiller, Princeton University Press.

lower their prices and even sell at a loss. The first perception that the price of housing is dropping is reinforcing. Lots of people try to get rid of housing before it drops further. And homeowners with mortgages find that they have negative equity in their homes: their homes are now worth less than the money they borrowed to purchase them. The bank is unable to refinance on generous terms, and homeowners have no incentive to sacrifice to pay. Better to just leave, mail in the keys, and rent cheap.

But what made the collapse of the recent housing boom so extraordinary in its destructive effects? It was the transformation and multiplication of mortgage debt and other debt into what were supposed to be solid assets. And when the assets of banks were dominated by these ersatz creations, and when they were exposed for what they were, the banks started to go bankrupt. The multiplication process went through three phases.

Multiplication I

Banks invented a way of turning risky assets into gold. You bundle a lot of promises to pay together on the grounds that while any particular homeowner who owes on a mortgage may default, the percentage of a whole group of homeowners who default will be low. The bundle is called a collateralized debt obligation (CDO). The original CDOs were mostly bundles of mortgages, but soon credit card debt and automobile debt ranging from safe (owed by the affluent) to less safe (owed by the almost poor) were tossed in as well. You make sure the components of CDOs sample all areas of the country, so that they are not subject to regional recessions. If all the debts were concentrated in Pennsylvania, rising unemployment in Pennsylvania might cause a lot of defaults and sink the CDO

People are asked to invest in a CDO on say four levels of risk (the levels are called tranches). There is a trade-off between risk and returns. If the CDO makes the sort of profit expected (most people keep making their mortgage and credit card payments), every level gets paid. But let us assume the profit is less than expected. Whatever profit exists is used to pay Level A first, and since they are taking the least risk, they get the lowest rate of return, although one substantially above bank interest. Level B is the next paid and gets a bit better rate, the same kind of trade-off for Level C. Level D gets paid last, and therefore when they get paid, they receive the highest rate of return. If the CDO shows a loss, nobody gets paid, and the losses have to be made good. The lower levels have to absorb losses first, but even if losses do not reach the top levels, everyone realizes they have lost their money. They own a worthless asset whose returns are problematic, and therefore, they cannot sell it (who would want to buy it?) to recoup their investment.

Multiplication II

Big investment banks wanted to carry on these operations outside the laws that regulate banks. All they had to do was set up a creature and call it a structured investment vehicle (SIV). The SIV would then borrow from the bank, buy the assets needed, and then do the actual bundling of those assets into a CDO. This was not so bad, but these banks by another name took the next step. They began to buy CDOs from other banks and manipulate them. For example, they might take the more risky levels of several CDOs and merge them into what was called a CDO squared. You would think that the offspring would be risky compared to its parents, but the notion was that you were spreading the risk. How likely was it that a whole collection of CDOs would all begin to show a loss? So now you could bet against that happening on various levels of potential risk and profit. It is not so much that CDOs squared had to be more risky. But now the jumble of assets that lay behind them was so complex that it was getting to be more difficult to evaluate them.

Multiplication III

It is only normal to want to take out insurance on any investment to guard against loss, which is to say against the possibility that the CDO or CDO squared shows no profit, and you have a worthless asset. The American International Group (AIG) is an insurer based in America with operations in 130 countries and is the 18th largest public company in the world. It began to allow the owners of securities to insure themselves against loss by taking out an insurance policy called a credit default swap. But it wanted to escape the regulations that govern ordinary insurance. Therefore, you bought an agreement such that if your security defaulted (did not pay its return), AIG would pay you its face value in something solid, such as cash or Treasury bonds.

Then, AIG did something extraordinary: it allowed people to take out the same policy on the same security, even if they did not own it. It thought this was good business. If it sold enough policies on enough securities, what was the chance they would all default? It was like giving earthquake insurance in an area in which there were likely to be no earthquakes. Eventually the worth of the policies of non-owners was 30 times the worth of the policies of owners. Thus was invented a way of multiplying risk without limit. It is as if everyone in a town took out an insurance policy on everyone else; and the company got its calculation of risks wrong because it accepted inflated medical assessments. Europe and Asia joined in the paper multiplication of assets: by June 2008, the total book value of "financial derivatives" was $684 trillion, more than 12 times the world's gross domestic product.

It would be wrong to overemphasize the impact of AIG. Borrowing on one asset to buy another (this is called leveraging) made its own contribution to the size of this mountain of "assets." Banks not only created risky securities but also believed they were sound. They bought CDOs from one another to transform them into CDOs squared. To do this, they would borrow from one another offering their own CDOs as security. This meant that everyone was increasing their "assets" by giving each other potentially worthless paper that they themselves had created. Every bank is linked to dozens of other banks in a complex web of buying and borrowing. There is nothing new in this. But it means that faith in one another is crucial.

The House Comes Tumbling Down

All it took to bring this rickety structure down was a downturn in the housing market. Some people with subprime mortgages and too much debt could not meet their payments, and others with negative equity in their homes had no incentive to do so. The CDOs dropped in value. Assume a bank had borrowed 97% of the market value of its CDOs, and they dropped 5%. Now, they had negative equity, and the bank was stuck with bad assets. Ironically, it was now in the position of people who had taken out subprime mortgages at the height of the housing boom. When the price of homes started to drop, you found you owed more on your home than it was worth. When a large percentage of derivatives were shown to be risky rather than sound, banks found themselves with debts larger than the value of their assets. They had negative equity, but they could not simply vacate their premises and mail the keys to someone.

Banks with bad assets cannot lend. They will not even engage in cash transfers with other banks whom they suspect of also hiding worthless assets. No one can borrow for houses, tuition, business expenses, and employers go under, and unemployment escalates. People who are frightened and broke spend less, and the retail and service sectors lose. Retirement funds and charities find their investments worth less, some by as much as 50%. What starts with bankrupt banks sends the whole economy into a recession.

AIG (the insurer) was itself on the verge of bankruptcy. Hedge funds are buyers who purchase securities with the capital of very wealthy investors. They often made bets with AIG against the soundness of a particular security. This was really a bet on their own expertise, for example, that they could predict the fate of sections of the stock market or the market as a whole. A few were very shrewd. They bought AIG promises to pay but sold them when the market was buoyant. They were among the few who were reinterpreting the message of the ratings. They saw that many securities labeled AAA were really risky and realized that the whole edifice might collapse. They knew that if there was a collapse, all policies would be suddenly presented for payment, AIG would go broke, and no one would get paid. So they sold off their policies to the "gullible" at a profit.

Actually, AIG went broke before most securities began to default. To inspire confidence in its ability to pay, it agreed to put aside large sums as collateral if its rating went below AA. As the collapse began, even the rating agencies saw AIG was at risk and downgraded it below AA. AIG just did not have the large sums it needed to set aside. It was too big to be allowed to go under, and the public was panicking by then, so the US government "gave" it $85 billion so it could meet its obligations.

This might seem enough to save the hedge funds who hold agreements to pay with AIG. If the government will stand behind its ability to pay, what is the problem? The problem is that the sums AIG needs to meet its obligations may grow to a point beyond which the government is willing to pay, or at least willing to pay enough to give you the full purchase price of your security. Therefore, there is no confidence that the agreements with AIG are sound, so no one is willing to buy them, which means their market value is zero. Many hedge funds went bankrupt and took their investors down with them.

The Rating Agencies

This tale makes it clear that none of these levels of multiplication would have been possible without assessment inflation. On all levels, securities that were actually risky were getting AAA ratings. Here enter the big five credit rating agencies that do the assessing: A. M. Best, Fitch, Moody's, Standard and Poor's, and Egan Jones. They issue ratings like AAA (blue chip), AA (medium low risk), A (well, still low risk), BBB (medium risk), BB (speculative), B (watch out), and C (why not take a ticket on the lottery). They gave inflated ratings to the CDOs squared, which poses two questions: why did their standards slip, and why did others not perceive that ratings were inflated and reinterpret their message? If AAA was being used too liberally, alert people should have said to themselves that it no longer meant blue chip but rather appreciable risk.

The Balance of Power Between Rating Agencies and the Banks

Banks go to the rating agencies for good ratings before they issue their securities. If they are to get a bad rating, what is the point of trying to sell? There is the added bonus that if the agency gives it a high rating, it is less likely to downgrade it later on because that is an admission that they were wrong. The pressure is on the rating agencies to satisfy their customers; if not, the latter will simply go to another more lenient agency and never come back. Several things seem quite incredible. Rating agencies only get paid if the bank or company decides to use the rating. The banks bargain with them: if I make this change to the CDO, will you give it AAA? Banks actually hold stock in the rating agencies. In addition, the salaries and prestige of those employed by big investment banks appeal to agency staff, and they often hope to get jobs with them in the future. They do not want to be blacklisted by the merchant banks for having done them a disservice.

A rating agency must not incur costs that its competitors avoid. Securities had got very complicated. To go into every mortgage, credit card, and so forth in the package that lies behind a CDO squared would be time-consuming and expensive. What bank is going to pay you for the cost of that? Therefore, you will assess risk by models that are cheap to run.

The models themselves were too optimistic. Recall that CDOs merged mortgages from all parts of the nation on the assumption that while there might be a drop in house prices in one area, there would not be a general downturn. In fact, when banks merged the more risky levels of CDOs into CDOs squared, the mortgages included often became less diverse in terms of area. The CDOs squared also included automobile and credit-card debt. The models predicted that housing and automobile and credit-card debt would not default collectively, but rather relied on statistics showing that one kind of default seemed fairly independent of the others. Therefore, even a moderate downturn in housing should not have disastrous general effects. In fact, the value of housing was so crucial, and the chance of a general downturn so high, that the model assumptions were wrong.

It would be nice if the models had been altered to take account of different assumptions about interdependence (this can be done by what is called Bayesian statistics). Emails have been made public, which show that some modelers were aware of what they were doing. To one another, they said that a CDO could be structured by a cow and get rated, and expressed the hope that they would all be retired by the time this house of cards comes down.

The men at the top frowned them away. Their bosses did not want to confront the law of assessment inflation. They would have had to say to themselves: positive assessments will tend to crowd out negative assessments if those assessed are more powerful than the assessors. Has not the fact our rating agency must compete with other agencies for bank customers allowed the banks to influence our thinking, and predisposed us to give them the inflated ratings they want? Their bosses would need to have become more critical about their own psychology, and employers rarely like employees who tell them to do that.

Banks are not the only customers that seek assessments. Businesses go to a rating agency to determine the risks of trading with someone else. If I agree to supply x with so many reams of paper, what is the chance x will default? At this point, the rating agency must be cautious because its reputation is at stake. A faulty assessment will quickly bring an angry client back to their premises. In other words, there was an inhibiting factor that fought against the tendency for positive assessments to crowd out negative assessments. Why is it that rating agencies inflated their assessments so much over the last 10 years as compared to the past?

The most obvious explanation is that there was a tipping point. The balance of their customers tipped toward big investment banks and away from advising businesses. In 2006, Moody's reported that 44% of its revenue came from rating complex securities, while only 32% came from its traditional business of rating corporate bonds. The investment banks may not have been as numerous as the general run of businesses. But they were far more powerful in affecting the income of the rating agency.

Who has an Incentive to Reinterpret the Message?

The average person who seeks assessment of securities goes not to a rating agency but to a broker for advice as to what to buy. Brokers make their livings out of transactions and will always tend to underestimate risk. The public colludes: almost everyone wants to believe that there is an investment out there that is safe and will pay more than bank interest or the interest on Treasury bonds. During this period, securities were particularly tempting because interest rates were low. China and Europe were buying lot of US

Treasury bonds and notes, so there was no need to raise interest rates to attract buyers. The Treasury raises bank interest rates primarily to control inflation by encouraging savings over spending. Thanks to an influx of cheap manufactured goods from abroad, there was little inflation.

In sum, when assessments are inflated, all of the actors have incentive systems that discourage reinterpretation of what a grade of AAA means. The broker and his clients certainly do. As for the heads of investment banks, they are even less likely to reinterpret than the heads of the rating agencies. Most are self-deluded before they go to the rating agencies. When the agency says you were correct in seeking an AAA rating, you are reassured, simply ignoring the fact that you did your best to influence the outcome.

Why the Insiders did not Care

A few who worked for investment banks were shrewd and knew that the assessments of securities were inflated and that the risk was great. But it was in their interest to keep the reinterpretation of the message of AAA to themselves. Over 10 years, by creating and buying risky securities, you increase the volume of your bank's business and it reaps huge profits. Therefore, you are paid salary and bonuses of $3 000 000 per year amounting to $30 000 000 over the decade. It is true that eventually your decisions render the assets of your firm worthless. But you were not silly enough to invest your $30 000 000 in your own bank and go down with it. You invested in high-yield bonds and traded these for safe Treasury notes, the moment you saw signs of a recession.

So what do you care? You will not share the lot of the ordinary person or the ordinary investor. Your home, savings, and retirement fund will not disappear in the general collapse. You may lose your job. But you are far better off than if a conservative investment policy had got you a miserable income of $1 000 000 per year.

15

What is to be Done?

Key Concept: (13) Market (regulation of the market). *What steps and regulatory institutions are needed to avoid future crises like that of 2008?*

Preview: *What ought to have been done; never again; expert opinion; misleading information as a tradable item; roots of the crisis of 2011; will the US economy collapse?*

When the crisis struck Obama got off to a bad start. The administration's recovery package included tax cuts to the non-wealthy so they could pay their bills and make purchases, and funds earmarked to finance useful public works (roads, bridges, flood control, green energy). This was simply not enough to address the roots of the problem, namely, how to fight unemployment immediately, how to get the banks working again immediately, and how to give immediate relief to people losing their homes.

What Ought to have been Done

Obama may well have been hampered by political restraints, but I am not and therefore, can say what I think ought to have been done ideally.

Huge grants to the states would have meant they would not have to had lay off thousands of employees. This suggestion got lost in the political process. Americans needed some respite before the spending on public works came into play, which always entail a lag of some six to eighteen months. The banks should have been nationalized, as Britain did in 2008

How to Improve Your Mind: Twenty Keys to Unlock the Modern World,
First Edition. James R. Flynn.
© 2012 John Wiley & Sons, Ltd. Published 2012 by John Wiley & Sons, Ltd.

and as Sweden did in its crisis of 1992. You could then look at their books, buy up their worthless assets, and give them the money they needed to start making loans again. At that that point, with guarantees against losses, private capital would start investing in banks. The Obama administration talked about attracting private capital but did not do the things necessary to make anyone believe that banks were good investments.

When buying up "worthless assets," the houses that now had a market value below what was owed on them should have been treated as the property of the bank. The government would buy them from the bank at the market price. The banks were hardly in a position to drive a hard bargain; after all, they were dependent on the government to give them extra money well beyond the worth of their assets. The government would now have a large stock of state owned housing and would rent them to former owners that qualified. The affluent can walk away happy that they are debt free. Those below a certain income can rent their former home at 25% of their income, in many cases unemployment benefits. When they get a job or a decent job, they can start to regain ownership by raising their payments and building up equity in their home.

During the housing boom, in order to increase home ownership, the government put pressure on banks to give subprime mortgages to poor people, people whose ability to meet their payments was doubtful. It is wrong to single this out as the main cause of the crisis of 2008. It was only one cause of the housing boom. And what made the collapse of that boom so fraught was banks peddling CDOs and rating agencies giving those securities AAA ratings. No one forced them to pretend that subprime mortgages were good investments.

However, state housing is the obvious solution to the subprime mortgage problem. They put people with low wages and intermittent employment into homes without mortgages of any sort and without any risk of default. State housing simply banishes the need for subprime mortgages and their attendant risks disappear.

Never Again

As for other measures to guard against a future collapse, regulation could dictate that a bank make a deposit when it issues a mortgage. The money would be forfeited if the mortgage is foreclosed and investigation revealed that the terms were likely to be beyond the buyer's means. However, the big problem is, what to do about the big five credit rating agencies and the danger of assessment creep?

One solution is to have a public body assess the ratings of the ratings agencies and rein them in. The big five would have to submit a list of all the securities they approved with the rating attached (a matter of public record anyway) and all of those cases in which they were approached but no rating was accepted. The agencies would know that if the latter category were nil, they would be subject to deep suspicion. Banks would be obliged to inform the public body of the subsequent history of the security, that is, if it was taken to another rating agency and what modifications were made. They would be warned against the fiddle of holding that the security was a "new" security with no past history, and the history of the security would have to be sent to the new rating agency. Each year a random sample of the securities rated by an agency would be investigated in depth.

You would examine corporations and CDO packages, of course. But vitally important would be scrutiny of the new financial instruments that the banks will inevitable invent to render assessment more complex and less rigorous. At the end of the exercise, if your average rating happens to be substantially below that of the agency's ratings, all of its securities over that year would be automatically downgraded by that amount.

There is a naivety in all of this. It may seem that the public body should be safe from capture by investment banks in a way the rating agencies themselves were not. After all, the banks are not customers who can subvert it by withholding their custom. However, the assessed are still many and powerful, while the assessor is one and in terms of political influence, relatively weak. The capture of regulatory bodies by those they are supposed to regulate dominates US history. The fact that this body has draconian penalties, that is, can downgrade the ratings provided at a stroke, merely means that companies and banks will mobilize all of their powers to pack its membership with compliant representatives of the corporate world and try to co-opt those who are initially resistant.

To defend independence, there are three weapons at our disposal: locate responsibility as close to the President as possible; isolate the regulators from the world of the regulated; create a culture of resistance.

The President should be made directly responsible for safeguarding the independence of what I will call the "Council of Credit Rating Assessment." Its head should be appointed by the President and responsible directly to his Chief of Staff who would give the President frequent reports. In other words, Presidential supervision of the Council should be diluted by a minimum of intermediaries. There should be a tradition that the President discusses his or her (no luck yet) nominee with ten members of Congress, five appointed by each party, opening the meeting with, "do you think this person can be trusted to be strong and independent?" He need not get their unanimous consent, but the event would insure that the appointment would attract publicity and debate and if the President were to appoint someone who proved compliant, there would be many who could say I told you so.

Upon appointment, the Council's staff would take a course of lectures on the history of the capture of regulatory bodies and how new financial instruments had outwitted assessors. This would be a statement that we mean to be different. All communications to and from the corporate world, calls, letters, emails, and social contacts, would have to be logged, just as a policeman has to reveal any contact with criminals. This would not be so much effective in itself as to serve as a daily reminder of the mission and culture of the organization. The experts hired would include accountants with auditing experience, mathematicians, and finance economists.

Senior staff intending to stay for life should get attractive retirement and pay packages. When junior staffers discover irregularities, they should be given very large bonuses. The financial world has a charming habit of blacklisting for life any government employee who seriously inconveniences them. The records of those the financial world attempts to recruit should be thoroughly scanned. Those who leave would not be allowed to take posts that might imply a prior conflict of interest (a promised bribe), which is to say they would be under "supervised employment" (only take jobs that are approved) for 10 years.

The Experts Think and Talk

All of this may merely make capture a slow process, but even that is worth while. For help, I turned to the fall 2008 issue of *International Economy*. It gives the views of the editors and 14 experts as to how we might avoid over-rated securities in the future. The two editors are crippled by ignorance of the law of assessment inflation. They say we should disenfranchise the present rating agencies and spawn "a myriad of small, more agile, more inventive" risk investment services. These small assessors may well give good advice to firms that want to know the risk of doing business with someone else. But when an investment bank with securities to rate approaches them, the bank's clout as a customer will corrupt these smaller agencies even more easily than it corrupted the large rating agencies that exist at present. And with an anarchy of multiple ratings out there, people will tend to ask their broker whether the stock has been rated properly and thus rely on the worst assessor possible.

The 14 experts are divided into three groups. Some say make assessing the monopoly of a governmental agency or at least give the Securities and Exchange Commission (SEC) greater power to regulate the market. Next there are those who rightly say that the SEC is an excellent example of capture by the corporations it is supposed to regulate, that any government agency will meet the same fate, and that therefore nothing can be done. I have tried, of course, to find a middle path between these two that might do some good for a long time. The others say nothing much at all. In sum, I do not think there is an awareness of what must be done to prevent a re-occurrence of the crisis of 2008.

Some of the experts love the kind of jargon that prevents them from educating the public. For example, one says "rating agencies play an important role by reducing informative asymmetry" but says little about how to make them do their job (see Box 15.1). When a distinguished journalist (Robert Fisk) addressed a distinguished university, academics asked him what they could do to make their work relevant to a broader public. Fisk replied, "Stop writing such poisonous prose." The students present gave him tumultuous applause. The academics remained mute. They are caught in a bind because journals dismiss their submissions unless expressed in the convoluted language that shows that you are "up with the state of play." It is a pity that more than a lack of concepts cheats thousands of people of their opportunity to be critical observers of their time.

Box 15.1   Poisonous prose

Just to decode the phase "reducing information asymmetry," take a market in which the owner of a good used car knows its condition, but potential buyers are ignorant. They will assume that its condition is the average of all used cars for sale and, indeed, suspect that it is a lemon. Therefore, they will offer a price below what the owner knows it to be worth and owners with really good used cars will withdraw from the market. Now, the average condition of used cars for sale drops further, and the same

---

thing will happen to what are now the best cars for sale – until no decent car is offered for sale at all. The only things for sale will be lemons. The economist who developed the theory received a number of requests for his paper from those interested in the market for lemons.

Now, apply this to securities. Everyone knows that merchant banks will not give accurate information as to their value, so the same dynamic would mean that the only securities offered would be lemons. So, by giving an objective rating of securities, the rating agencies would eliminate the "information asymmetry" and ensure that buyers could choose between securities that ranged from safe (cars) to risky and make an informed choice. A pity they did not do their job.

Misinformation as a Tradable Item

The helplessness of the unregulated market to guard against tragedies like the crisis of 2008 is manifest. It is a special case of something we said at the start: the market itself cannot define what is a tradable item. Providing false information can be very profitable, at least for those who sell it and, for a time, even for those who buy it, if the "information" enhances the value of their assets (witness the profits made out of CDOs squared). It is easy to forget that we already regulate the flow of information to guard against injustice and personal tragedy. We try to forbid insider trading (someone inside a corporation knows whether it will soon issue a good or bad statement about its profits, and can therefore make a killing by buying or selling its stock). We try to protect consumers from those who try to sell them a car that is unsafe or a house that is a firetrap. It is time to protect banks from their own folly.

Despite the recent past, we hear much from those who ask us to believe that regulation of the stock market is irrational and counterproductive. The only antidote is people like you and me learning enough about how markets operate to suspect their motives. The great John Maynard Keynes is on our side: "When the capital development of a country becomes a by-product of the activities of a casino, the job is likely to be ill-done." (Keynes, 1936, chapter 12, section VI).

The Crisis of 2011

As readers will know, we are now in the grip of another financial crisis. In part, it is a consequence of the crisis of 2008. Governments had to borrow money to give to the banks and restore their solvency. Actually, the US government has been repaid most of that money (the major exception is what it loaned to the automotive industry). Its main problem is that since it did not stimulate its economy sufficiently, it has slow growth and high unemployment. Thus, it has reduced tax revenue, and the almost $4 trillion lost on foreign wars has not helped.

Some European nations are worse off. They still suffer from the huge debts they contracted, and they have weak economies that never recovered at all from the 2008 recession (with consequent loss of tax revenue). Germany is an exception, in that she attained a healthy rate of growth as early as 2010. Greece is the worst off, because she added fiscal irresponsibility to the mix (just kept spending as revenue declined).

US and European banks now have a new set of assets that have turned toxic. They advanced loans to governments that seemed safe but are now in danger of default. So, there may be another international banking crisis, and this time fewer nations are in a position to give banks money they need to survive.

Will the US Economy Collapse?

Europe may bring many US banks down, no matter what America does, but all the more reason to try to expand the economy as much as she can. The political paralysis that crippled America in July 2011 frightened many. It appeared that deadlock between those who wanted expenditure cuts now and those who wanted them later (after the economy revived) would paralyze the government and prevent America from paying the interest on its debts and even government salaries. The political parties reached a compromise that, if anything, made matters worse. At a time when the economy was stagnant and unemployment over 9%, the government was forbidden to stimulate the economy by new spending to create jobs. It takes a growing economy to generate the money needed to repay debt, and freezing economic growth ensures that the economy would be stagnant for some time.

Lurking in the background is the fact that America is dependent on foreign investors to subsidize her debt. China plays a major role. She invests two-thirds of her savings in America by buying US Treasury bonds and other securities. Federal Reserve Chairman Ben Bernanke put Chinese dollar holdings at $2 trillion as of the end of 2010. However, there appears to be no immediate danger that foreign investors will withdraw their money.

Even now, people around the world fear that their nations are more likely to default on their debts than the US Treasury and therefore buy its bonds. As long as Chinese exports to America exceed the value of what she imports, she virtually has to loan America the difference, so that America has the money to pay for her exports. Nonetheless, someday the limits of economic dependence may be reached. China, in order to avoid recession, is doing less saving and is spending on additional public works to stimulate her economy. She may simply not have the surplus America needs.

A bald summary: bankrupt banks (and the ensuing recession) caused government debt; bankrupt governments now threaten to cause bank debt (government default on their notes). Where both government and banks are bankrupt, the country must be bailed out by other nations. If other nations do not, their own banks will be threatened, and this time, they will have fewer resources to bail their own banks out. Chinese investment cannot prop up the whole system. It may not be much comfort, but I hope market analysis has helped you understand why we may see the most serious world depression since the great depression of the 1930s. By the time this book appears, you should know the outcome.

Reference

Keynes, J.M. (1936) *The General Theory of Employment, Interest, and Money,* Palgrave Macmillan, Basingstoke.

Part 4
Enemies of Science

16

Reality – What Scientists Really Say About Science

Anti-Key: **(14) Reality is a text**. *The next three chapters are an attempt to immunize you against Anti-Keys or concepts that impede rationality and critical thinking. I will begin with a critique of the notion that science cannot claim to tell us the truth about human behavior and the physical universe.*

Preview: *Reality is a text; perceptions of reality; constructs of reality; the nature of scientific progress; what the philosophers said; the sociology of knowledge; Immanuel Kant; multiple interpretations of reality; how truth relativity self-destructs; hatred for a word; even muddled minds can teach us something.*

I assume that none of you are addicted to pseudo-sciences like astrology. Carl Sagan, the Cornell astronomer, pointed out that while the planets and stars are very large, they are merely collections of dirt, metals, gas, and so forth, and unlikely to influence our fate. They are also very far away. If anyone really believes that the position of material objects at the time of their birth is important, the furniture in the room, while small, is very close. The exact position of tables, chairs, lamps, and so forth is obviously far more relevant. If this does not disabuse you, I am not sure what to say.

However, if you have attended a university over the last 40 years, you may well be confused about whether there is such a thing as the real world, and whether science is the best method of learning about it.

How to Improve Your Mind: Twenty Keys to Unlock the Modern World,
First Edition. James R. Flynn.
© 2012 John Wiley & Sons, Ltd. Published 2012 by John Wiley & Sons, Ltd.

Reality is a Text

This phrase has become popular as the rallying cry of those who deny that there is a real world that science explores. The implication is that we create reality, indeed, that the multitude of human beings creates multiple realities when each casts his own or her own web of words or ideas around the world. How are people led to doubt that there is such a thing as one real world in which all human beings live? I believe that there is one physical universe in which other people and myself reside and that it existed long before people did (for about 13 billion years) and will exist long after we are all gone.

The notion that reality is subjective arises out of a series of misunderstandings that reinforce one another. These number at least five. There are misunderstandings about: the fact that perceptions of reality vary; that constructs people use to make sense of reality vary; that the history of science shows one theory after another being replaced; that philosophers of science say things like, "science cannot establish the truth about the universe"; and the sociology of knowledge. The last shows that science exists only in a particular kind of society, which is taken to prove that it is only "relative."

Perceptions of Reality

There is no doubt that different creatures and different people have different perceptions of the real world. A blind person cannot see the heavens, and a starfish cannot see much of anything at all. Nonetheless, those with normal human vision perceive the world more fully than other people, and the latter pay a price for their less adequate perceptions. Only sighted people would have invented astronomy, be aware of a large asteroid approaching the earth, and be in a position to deflect it. If we cannot deflect it, the blind and the starfish will die just as readily as the rest of us. They share our fate because there is a real world in which real events occur, and they live in it just as much as we do.

Some are afflicted by perceptions that give them inaccurate information about the real world. A person in the desert about to die of thirst may have a hallucination that shows an oasis just ahead. If the hallucination is powerful enough, it may persist right up to the point that he scoops up water to drink, but what he will get is a mouthful of sand. Failure to perceive the real world accurately always takes its toll.

Constructs of Reality

Our notion of the real world does not consist of simple perceptions. We make sense of the world by using theories, that is, systems of concepts that assert relations of cause and effect. By testing theories systematically against experience, science affords a far better picture of reality than any competitor.

The Dobu Indians posit a world governed by magic and malevolence. If your farm starts to yield fewer yams, you assume your neighbor is using charms, so that your yams walk over to his field during the night. The best way to stop him is to poison him. We would do a soil analysis and perhaps find one-crop farming is sapping the fertility of the soil and that rotation of crops is the answer. If the Dobus shared our scientific approach, there would be fewer hungry Dobus.

The constructs of pre-industrial peoples always include the empirical method of observation, which is of course the proto-type of science. If they did not use this when it counts, they would not survive. For example, they observe when fish are usually present and cast their nets at that time. They master reality when they anticipate the scientific method, and fail to do so when they use something else.

In passing, ordinary logic is so successful in helping us to interpret reality that you cannot find any people who do not use it. They may have false premises and therefore reach false conclusions, for example: only magic can move yams; my yams are gone; therefore, they have been moved by magic. But when they depend on observation for their premises, they tend to reach reliable conclusions necessary to sustain life. In the stone-age cultures of New Guinea, if children ask why they should not eat something, an adult will say, that is a poisonous guibble. Perfect logic: all guibbles are poisonous; that is a guibble; therefore, that is poisonous. People can refuse to use logic, but to the extent that they do, they handicap their ability to interpret reality.

The Nature of Scientific Progress

Misunderstandings about the history of science confuse people. There is ample evidence that science sometimes gets stalled unless there is a "paradigm-shift." For example, Newton's mechanical explanation of the heavens in terms of forces operating is simple space and time was very successful. As a result, some scientists said that they would take no astronomical theory seriously unless they could build a model of it in a machine shop. Problems with Newton's gravitational theory were treated as if the paradigm had to be true. For example, Newton's equations gave predictions for the orbit of Mercury that were not quite right. But if you were locked into his theory, you tried to explain them away: perhaps there was a planet closer to the Sun than Mercury, one difficult to see, that pulled it out of orbit. One astronomer even thought he saw a planet (he saw a sunspot), named it Vulcan, and received a medal from the Academy of Dijon.

As Einstein pointed out, you had to shatter the mechanical paradigm before you could propose a new alternative theory, and without an alternative theory, things Newton could not explain would be swept under the carpet. Scientists would think of them as puzzling but trivial and assume that the answer would be found. Eventually. Einstein shattered the mechanical paradigm. He posited that the shape of space, rather than forces, could influence orbits and that the shape of space altered in the vicinity of the heavenly bodies. When you drop a heavy ball on to a blanket, it creates a funnel shape. The Sun creates a funnel shape in the space in its vicinity, and the planets revolve around that funnel without falling into the Sun (they are moving too fast). And lo and behold, when you measure the shape of the funnel very close to the Sun, where Mercury happens to be, you get the right orbit.

So, you often need a new paradigm for science to progress. But note that paradigms do not mean that science itself is "just a paradigm," something within which we are trapped with no access to any reality except what the paradigm defines as real. Paradigm shifts merely show how hard it is to invent radically new theories when the field is held by a very successful old theory. The scientific method uses evidence to test predictions, and that evidence is a real occurrence that takes place outside paradigms. And when there is a breakthrough from one paradigm to another, evidence tells us what theory gives a closer approach to reality.

What the Philosophers Said

Philosophers of science debate questions like, can we say that a scientific theory is true? When they answer in the negative, the unwary start talking about science as a perspective no more valid or true than any other perspective. Let us see what philosophers actually mean by this.

Karl Popper (1902–1994) pointed out that if we say that a particular theory is true, that seems to imply that any new theory would be false

(Popper, 1959). Moreover, how could we know a theory is true? We would have to know that all tests of the theory from now to the end of time would verify its predictions.

When we look at how science has actually progressed, we find that it is more helpful to say that we abandoned a theory when it was falsified in favor of an alternative theory that, thus far at least, had not been falsified. For example, there were two competing theories about combustion. One posited that certain things contained an element that made them flammable and then lost it when they burned. The other posited that things combined with something (oxygen) when they burned. The obvious test was to weigh things both before and after they burnt. They weighed more after they were burnt, so the first theory was falsified, and the oxygen theory was not. Science had progressed, but no one could go beyond saying that the oxygen theory had not been falsified thus far.

Imre Lakatos (1922–1974) pointed out that there was an ambiguity in saying that a theory had not been falsified (Lakatos, 1978). If the predictions of a theory have been falsified, you can patch it up by adding new ad hoc hypotheses. There was an astronomer at Harvard who, whether seriously or simply to make a point I do not know, showed that you could salvage Newton's falsified predictions of the orbit of Mercury by adding an assumption: the Sun's center of gravity shifted from its center to its surface when, and only when, Mercury was concerned. No reason could be given for this shift. That is why it is called an ad hoc hypothesis, meaning that its sole purpose was to save a theory from falsification after the event.

Lakatos therefore suggested that we should also assess scientific theories in terms of their fertility, that is, whether they suggest new and interesting questions. Newton's theory could be salvaged only if we spent a lot of time patching it up. The alternative theory of Einstein did not need patching up (it had not been falsified up to that time), but more important, rather than just spawning sterile ad hoc hypotheses, it suggested many new and exciting hypotheses. If space curved in the vicinity of stars, then when light traveled past a star, it was going through curved rather than straight-line space. Therefore, we would predict that the path of light would bend as it passed a star. That prediction proved correct. Doesn't that sound like his theory is closer to reality than Newton's theory?

So, do not be deceived by the fact that no scientific theory is true, and certainly do not be deceived by the fact that no scientific theory gives us a final and perfectly accurate picture of the universe. Neither means that science is "subjective" or merely one point of view among many. It merely means that science progresses towards a better understanding of reality, although without any guarantee we will ever attain perfect understanding. Our minds may be too limited to invent a fully fecund scientific theory.

The Sociology of Knowledge

Another influence that lends plausibility to the notion that all science is arbitrary is misunderstanding the significance of the sociology of knowledge.

It is quite true that everything we think has a social setting, including what we think needs to be known. Science requires that we distance ourselves from nature and ask questions about it. Zuni Indian culture assumed a universal harmony between man and nature so science could not possibly arise. Dobu culture assumed that every event was determined by magic, so they already knew all of the answers without science. Historians have argued that modern science, with its need for precise measurement, could not have flowered without the rise of capitalism. People who work in factories have to get to work on time, and that requires accurate clocks. Even the detail of scientific theories has a social setting. Greek society affected astronomy because of its obsession with circles (although they had reasons that seemed convincing at the time). Science is a cultural product just as much as magic.

However, historical or sociological relativism does not equal epistemological (or truth) relativism. Once we are fortunate enough to live in a society like classical Greece, we begin to invent fruitful hypotheses about the heavens. Once we live in a society not obsessed with circles, we can have a better astronomy that tells us more truths about the heavens. Once the scientific method has been invented, testing hypotheses against our observations leads us closer to reality. Progress exists even for something as "subjective" as numbers. It is incredibly cumbersome to multiply and divide if you use Roman numerals. Arabic numbers such as we use today make them easy. Even though we can give a sociological and historical account of the rise of Arabic numerals (the abacus was important), the fact remains: for everybody everywhere, they facilitate doing calculations.

Those who assert that the sociology of knowledge makes social science truth-relative contradict themselves. Sociology of knowledge itself arises only in a social setting; indeed, society has to be highly sophisticated. If that makes something unreliable, the sociology of knowledge is itself unreliable. Odd that ordinary sociology, say the sociology of the family, yields unreliable results but that the most difficult kind of sociology yields results that can be trusted.

146

Immanuel Kant

To this stew of misunderstanding, we must add a pinch of Kant (1724–1804). He distinguished between "things in themselves" that were beyond human experience and comprehension, and the "phenomenal world," the world we see around us through the spectacles of our human perceptual apparatus. Kant did not want to discredit science but wanted to put it on firmer foundations. He said that all people view the world through the same kind of spectacles; and therefore, we could all use science to arrive at shared and reliable conclusions about the events we perceive.

But particularly in Europe, modern thinkers decided that he was mistaken. Rather than a common pair of spectacles to view the unknowable reality, everyone had their own pair. Each paradigm has its own picture of reality, each philosopher their own subjective truth, each society its own world view. The final step, of course, was to hold that each person had their own point of view, and if you called every person's point of view a "text," then reality was simply a text subject to an infinite number of interpretations. The texts were not about reality: there was no such thing as reality. Each of us creates "reality" by writing our own text and casting it over the world. This is called postmodernism.

Multiple Interpretation of Reality

Derrida is the postmodernist par excellence and held in great esteem (Derrida, 1976). It is easier to diagnose what his followers believe than to discern what he believes. He won American adherents in 1966, when he delivered a lecture at Johns Hopkins University. He stated his thesis as follows:

> The entire history of the concept of structure, before the rupture of which we are speaking, must be thought of as a series of substitutions of center for center, as a linked chain of determinations of the center. Successively, and in a regulated fashion, the center receives different forms or names. The history of metaphysics, like the history of the West, is the history of these metaphors and metonymies. Its matrix . . . is the determination of Being as *presence* in all senses of this word. It could be shown that all names related to fundamentals, to principles, or to the center have always designated an invariable presence – *eidos, archē, telos, energeia*, (essence, existence, substance, subject), *alētheia*, transcendentality, consciousness, God, man, and so forth.

I will not compromise the luminous clarity of these words with comment. But the message the audience heard was that science was just one text among many; and therefore not a privileged approach to understanding.

Some 15 years ago, I directed a public letter to Derrida and asked him whether he actually believed something like that. I pointed out that his meaning was unclear and offered a list of four possibilities:

(1)   He did not believe that he and I inhabited a common physical universe.
(2)   He believed that, but thought that science had competitors in understanding that universe. Perhaps something like astrology or whatever he cared to name.
(3)   He accepted physical science, but thought that its methods could not be applied to human behavior in the form of social science.
(4)   He accepted that, but believed in some kind of extreme linguistic determinism, such as that our language determines what we perceive. For example, that people who have no word for orange will not perceive orange (I called this the "Whorf hypothesis," being ignorant that it goes beyond anything Benjamin Whorf endorsed).

I suggested that if he did not hold any of these views, he might want to say what "reality is a text" actually did mean. I received no reply (see Box 16.1).

Box 16.1   Mad men on the subway

This does not mean that he was at a loss for words. Such a thing is inconceivable. I suspect that he had better things to do with his time. Whatever his merits, his followers have much to answer for. There has been concern about the increasing number of people on New York subway trains that are clearly mad. They sit staring into space and constantly mumbling to themselves. Rumor has it (rumor can be misleading) that a NYU graduate student was assigned to record what they were saying. When the tapes were played, much amplified, their voices were audible for the first time. They were mumbling, "Reality is a text." They had been driven mad, not by fluorine in the water supply or too much sugar in the tomato paste, but by sitting in on university lectures.

As to why none of the four alternatives are viable:

(1) The local bus station is in the same place for Derrida and I, as evidenced by the fact that we will encounter one another if we both want a bus ride. If I gave him an out-of-date bus timetable, it would be a less reliable text that an up-to-date one. He would miss the bus.

(2) Every time he put on his spectacles, he verified that the theory of optics was a more valid text than competing theories. They explained why his spectacles worked. Nothing else did.

(3) When William Sumner, the great pioneer sociologist, visited Boston, he found the Anglican clergy were brooding about the fact that most of the prostitutes in Boston were Anglicans. Their hypothesis was that there must be some subliminal message in their sermons that was corrupting morals. Sumner noted that the Anglican Church ran the orphanages in Boston and that their graduates were nominal Anglicans. He hypothesized that girls raised in an impersonal environment were more likely to be demoralized and become prostitutes. His hypothesis was fruitful. It predicted that if the Catholic Church ran the orphanages in New Haven, a disproportionate number of prostitutes would be nominal Catholics. In sum, Sumner's "text" had more explanatory power than that of the Anglican clergy.

(4) If you offer strong incentives to people whose languages have no word for orange, they will pick it out on a color spectrum (being a bit more uncertain at the margins). We have never encountered a people whose language was a serious barrier to establishing common locations for objects.

How Truth Relativity Self-Destructs

When postmodernists write about their doctrines, are those not texts? If all texts lack reliability, why should anyone trust their texts? And if texts are subject to an infinite number of interpretations, will they wear an interpretation that what they are saying is "that the cow jumped over the moon"? How can they exempt their own works as having reliability and one correct meaning without being entirely arbitrary?

Postmodernists are really in the untenable position that Plato put Heraclitus. When Heraclitus said that "all was in flux," Plato replied that the words he had just uttered might be in flux, but the flux was not enough to worry about. Otherwise how was it that their meanings were stable enough so that we could all understand them? The only consistent behavior for a complete truth relativist is to remain mute. In this case, that might not be a bad thing. At present, they talk and write, and confuse staff and students in departments ranging from Anthropology to Sociology, from History to Gender studies, from English to Film Studies. They do less harm in the last pair in that the subject matter really does consist of texts or at least human creations. Even there, they still confuse. An infinite number of interpretations of Hamlet are not viable: it is not about a teenager suffering from acne.

Hatred for a Word

If you dislike the word "reality" for some idiosyncratic reason, you can substitute something else that does the same job. You can say that certain percepts or scientific theories are more "reliable" than others, meaning that they predict our experiences more accurately. You can then deny that there is such a thing as reality. Humanity is trapped in the world of their perceptions and their constructs; but some percepts and theories are more "adequate" in accounting for those experiences.

In other words, when I distinguish between percepts and theories in terms of one telling us more about reality than others, you simply call the first construct-SUB-1, which is a construct in which events are more predictable, and the second construct-SUB-2, which is a construct in which events are less predictable. You have then avoided using the hated word "reality." But you have smuggled in the key distinction between the scientific worldview and non-scientific ones nonetheless. To do so, you have had to use complicated language that I do not care to imitate.

Even Muddled Minds can Teach us Something

The fact that we can learn nothing from postmodernism itself does not mean we can learn nothing from the people who call themselves postmodernists, or radical constructivists. First, some of them are highly intelligent, and intelligent people cannot help but say intelligent things. So, there will be insights hidden in their "texts," not because of their philosophical approach but despite it. No philosopher today accepts Hegel's philosophy of

150

the Absolute. But Hegel said a lot of insightful things not because he was a Hegelian but because he was so bright.

Second, the different perceptions human beings have of the world and of their selves are influential. Later on, we will see that even radical constructivists add something to the theory of international relations. The "texts" that people compose about their nations and other nations is essential to understanding their behavior. I think we always knew that. Long before post-modernism came along, scholars said that America's image of itself as special influenced its foreign policy. But maybe they did not give such factors sufficient weight.

If you are stuck with a post-modernist as a PhD supervisor, do not despair. Once you reject his or her confusions, you may salvage something from what he or she says. Sadly, when you write your dissertation you may have to preface the important stuff with some gibberish about texts, narratives, and so forth. But remember, after you get your degree, you can stop that and get on with what makes sense: using science to understand the real world without any apology.

References

Derrida, J. (1976) *Of Grammatology* (trans. G. C. Spivak), Johns Hopkins University Press, Baltimore, MD.

Lakatos, I. (1978) *The Methodology of Scientific Research Programmes: Philosophical Papers Volume 1*, Cambridge University Press, Cambridge.

Popper, K. (1959) *The Logic of Scientific Discovery*, Routledge, London.

17

History, Science, and Evolution – Only One Kind of Each

Anti-Keys: (15) Alternative histories; (16) Alternative sciences; (17) intelligent design. *If you believe in multiple interpretations of reality, it is logical to believe that there are different kinds of history and science of equal integrity. I will examine these claims on their merits. It is also claimed that here is an alternative to the theory of evolution, one that is in some sense more illuminating.*

Preview: *Writing better history; male history; male science; history and bias; history and legends; intelligent design; Darwin versus an absurd God; science and values; corrupting the youth.*

The notion that there are a variety of histories, all of equal status or all lacking any objective status, is pervasive among students of social science but by no means confined to them. If that were true, if no history was better than any other, it would be impossible for the writing of history to progress. Therefore, I will begin with an account of how "Western" history has improved over time.

Writing Better History

People get in the habit of writing down what happens to them (it is a wonderful aid to memory). But history is not about the texts people compose any more than a murder trial is about the transcript of the trial. Just as you want to know whether the accused actually did the

How to Improve Your Mind: Twenty Keys to Unlock the Modern World,
First Edition. James R. Flynn.
© 2012 John Wiley & Sons, Ltd. Published 2012 by John Wiley & Sons, Ltd.

murder, you want to know whether the Spanish actually sunk the battleship Maine (this was the excuse for America starting the Spanish–American War). Just as we may never achieve a perfect astronomy, so we may never achieve perfect history. But we may come closer and closer to a sophisticated account of what causes were really at work when events occurred.

Before Voltaire, aside from great exceptions such as the Greek historians, people tended to be hypnotized by prominent actors such as kings, queens, generals, and popes. Voltaire brought society into the account. He noted that these great men and women mobilized the resources of a society composed of people, and therefore, ordinary human beings and their lives and the human capital they supplied were rather important. Marx, with all his faults, made it impossible for historians to ignore the system of production and the classes it produced as crucial in history. Armies often make history, and the economy affects what kind of army is put into the field. People whose wealth is in horses tend to use cavalry; agricultural people produce the surplus to outfit a professional army of foot soldiers; the industrial revolution and modern nationalism allowed the state to draft a huge citizen army.

Within my own life time, the quality of history has improved enormously. Part of it is being more scrupulous about evidence. It is amusing to read the apologetic introductions authors write when a biography they published many years ago is republished. They are embarrassed by concocted events they added for "color" ("Mozart felt merry and sent a boy out to buy a bowl of punch") and by speculations as to what people must have been thinking ("As the captured Napoleon saw the shores of France fading into the distance, he must have thought of the glory he was leaving behind"). Today, one is assured that all thoughts are based on diaries and all conversations on transcripts.

Now that we see that history is the history of whole societies, all of our new sophistication about how societies work comes into play. When I was a child, I was taught that Charles the Great (742–814) was a charismatic figure whose military prowess had united France, Central Europe, and Italy into a semi-revival of the Roman Empire in the West: "Few could defy such a fierce and powerful leader." Today, the emphasis is on the discovery of a new method of plowing in Northern Europe. That gave Charles the surplus grain and the wealth needed to put a larger army in the field than his rivals. That surplus also allowed the feeding and breeding of larger horses, so that he had a cavalry the Southern Europeans could not match.

Male History

It has not been all progress. Student perceptions of history are clouded by talk of male history and feminist history, Western history and people's ownership of their own history, Pakeha (the Europeans of New Zealand) and Maori (the indigenous Polynesians) history, and so forth. There is no such thing as male history. If only males write history, they are likely to say too much about males and wear certain blinders. Both of these things make for bad history. If you leave out females, you leave out half the people who make up society. Males have a taste for war, and male historians may give generals a too prominent role.

Thanks to women historians, history is less limited in terms of whose contribution is taken into account (more about women's contribution) and in terms of the theories or spectacles that allow us to interpret events (more social history and less military). But that just produces better history, not some peculiar thing called "women's history." Good history, whoever writes it, must be scrupulous about evidence, and events should be interpreted in the light of the best social and natural science we have. That includes getting into the skins of people and seeing the world as they saw it. Men and women collectively are better at doing this than either alone. Therefore, history written by both men and women is better than it would be if either sex were writing it alone: Martians would do a very bad job of writing human history.

I do not want to stress "like empathizing with like" too much. All of us, through reading and imagination, can expand our powers of empathizing with others. Men can imagine what it is like for women to be raped. Even though I have never worked in a mine, I can imagine what it was like for a four-year-old to sit perched on a shelf for 12 h in the dark. Those who lack empathy often have an axe to grind. England had a guilty conscience about the Irish that made it necessary to dehumanize them. In *Punch*, Irish were portrayed, not as blacks, but as animals resembling chimpanzees (the Simian Celt). Some in the House of Lords preferred not to acknowledge the existence of the Great Famine. They said that the Irish were not starving but dying of the "green mouth disease." This was because, at the very last, people were desperate enough to eat grass, which made their mouths very green indeed.

Male Science

All I have said about "male history" is applicable to talk of male science, male medicine, and so forth. As we have seen, astronomy paid a price for the fact that Greeks and their admirers had something close to a monopoly. For hundreds of years, the Greek attachment to circles made it difficult to see that the planets simply did not move in circles. Progress occurred when Germans and Englishmen took over charting the heavens and when better data made circles untenable. But they did not invent a new kind of science that it makes sense to call German or English astronomy. They just invented better theories about what made the heavens work that had to be tested by the same scientific method used then and still used.

This is not to deny that we can make progress in terms of understanding the scientific method and how to use it. Even Galileo thought that the elegance of his mathematics and logic guaranteed the truth of his discoveries, and did not see that he had to test their predictions against experience. He said that he did experiments only to convince those who could not follow the mathematics.

Just like history, if only a limited group does science, it may suffer. Taking medicine as an example, more women doing research may bring an infusion of new theories, new hypotheses, more research into women's illnesses, and a new appreciation that treating the sick is an art, one that requires empathy and treatment of the whole person. But when testing theories and hypotheses, or performing follow-up studies of the effectiveness of treatment, the same scientific method will be applied, although perhaps with less bias in reading the results. Improving the practice of science does not give us an alternative science.

The Nazis did not think very clearly. Nonetheless, when they spoke of Jewish physics, even they did not mean that the Jews had invented an alternative to the scientific method. They meant that the Jewish scientists were so much more wicked than "Aryan" scientists that they distorted science for their own ends. For example, their minds were closed to what any true scientist could see, namely that the center of the earth was filled with ice (not some special kind of ice, just ordinary ice).

History and Bias

The fact that no history can be written without bias is supposed to be of great significance. The solution to this problem is to try to cut bias to a minimum. Reading a variety of accounts is a good start. For example, Jesus was after all a Jew, so it makes sense to read Jewish historians if one has been raised a Christian. Jewish historians see Jesus as a holy man, who did not think he was God or the Messiah. Rather, Jesus believed he had a mission to warn the Jews that the coming of the Messiah was near, and that they must purify themselves, not merely by obeying the letter of the law but by having charity in their hearts. Christian scholars challenge theses conclusions, of course. My point is only that we should all suspect that we are prey to bias and seek antidotes.

Everyone has a bias, but some are more biased than others. If a Jewish defendant is on trial, a Nazi Storm Trooper is less likely to be a reliable witness than a tolerant humane person known to be scrupulous about the truth. The fact that perfect history is not possible is no bar to being the best historian you can.

History and Legends

Peoples have their legends about their own past, but these are not histories of any sort, although a real historian may find something that is accurate within them. Most peoples are preliterate and have only oral accounts of the past, and we all know how things get distorted in the telling even if people are describing what they have all witnessed. There is a region of China where the people believe that they are, at least in part, descended from the troops of Alexander the Great. DNA testing shows that they are mistaken. However, legends can hold important clues about cultural evolution. Stories about goddesses may reveal an ancient matriarchal culture hidden behind the recent patriarchal one.

Some stress the fact that history has a different function for pre-industrial peoples. Whatever its accuracy, it is more "real" to them than any history a Western Historian could write. It gives them an image of their past that binds them together such as the myth that they are all descendants of a common great ancestor. It may reassure them about their place in the universe. Zuni legends stress their harmony with nature and the gods. Dobu legends relate them to the gods in the same way they relate to one another, a mixture of love and hate. What could be more real than that? What right do we have to project our notion of reality on to their culture?

The reply to this has been foreshadowed. Some pages ago, we allowed people to use words in an idiosyncratic way so long as distinctions were not lost. They could use constructs SUB-1 and constructs SUB-2 to distinguish theories that were more and less predictive of our experience, if they really wanted to talk that way. Now, we will let them use history SUB-1 and history SUB-2. The first is more real in the sense that it is about the events that actually happen to people over time, and the second is more real in the sense that it makes people feel more comfortable with the tenor of their lives. That is, it is more emotionally significant for them. It is the distinction we make when we say, "I want to know what really happened" on the one hand, and when we say, "I am really in love," on the other (see Box 17.1).

Box 17.1   Frozen at the stake

It is much easier to make people talk in odd ways than it is to make them behave strangely. Bertrand Russell commented on the limitations of even so savage a despot as Stalin. If Stalin said that fire freezes things and that cold burns them, everyone would have to comply on a verbal level. You would talk about putting something on the stove to "cool it" and putting it into the fridge to "heat it." But no one would actually put the teapot in the fridge when they boiled water for tea. It is just that anyone who did not mimic Stalin's language would be "frozen at the stake."

This should please those who have hang-ups about words. We have avoided the word-crime of saying that Western history is more real than folk history. Rather, we are saying that the two are simply different, real in such different senses that no comparison is implied. Fair enough, if you can be bought off so easily. Just so long as no one is so confused as to think that Western history is not a better "narrative" about what really happened.

Intelligent Design

Saint Thomas Aquinas argued that there could not have been an endless chain of causes receding into the past, but rather that there must have been an uncaused first cause that was the origin of all things including space and time. He based another of his arguments for the existence of God on the fact that the universe showed evidence of intelligent design. It would be surprising if these arguments were not resurrected today. The Big Bang theory posits a singularity whose "explosion" led to the entire universe we see around us and prior to which there was no space or time. The pattern of that explosion and the laws that governed what then occurred had to be delicately balanced to produce a universe of galaxies, stars, planets, and a planet that could support life. Some have argued that this implies the existence of an intelligence that crafted the whole with intent.

This is not a textbook on theology. I leave it to my readers to examine both the traditional and modern arguments for the existence of God. However, we must not confuse theology based on science with science itself. As we have seen, a scientific theory generates predictions that can be falsified, while theology does not.

Even if it were true that intelligent design lay behind the laws of our universe, that truth would add nothing to our knowledge of the content of those laws. Even when we can find no scientific explanation of some facet of the universe, the answer that it may be a product of intelligent design provides nothing that can be called a scientific explanation. Those who advocate intelligent design as an alternative to Darwin's theory of evolution, or creation "science" as an antidote to "godless" science, do not wish to recognize this because it means that their doctrines belong in a religion class rather than in a science class.

Darwin Versus an Absurd God

Darwin's theory explains why the hawk moth caterpillar has a rear end that looks like a snake's head (see Figure 17.1). Birds are the caterpillar's main predator, and birds are frightened of snakes. Originally, the resemblance to a snake was a chance thing, rare and approximate. But over many generations, caterpillars with the closest resemblance tended to survive to reproduce, and the resemblance became more accurate and came to dominate the species.

Whether adding that God wanted the rear end of a caterpillar to look like a snake enhances the dignity of God, I leave to those who think they know the mind of God. I think it makes God look absurd. But in any event, reading God's mind adds absolutely nothing to the scientific explanation.

Figure 17.1 The caterpillar that looks like a snake. Snake mimic hawkmoth caterpillar (*Hemeroplanes* sp.).
Photo © Dr George Beccaloni/Science Photo Library.

Darwin's theory is fruitful because it not only explains facts after the event, but also generates predictions precise enough to be tested. For example, if we found an isolated area where there were caterpillars and birds but no snakes, we would predict that the resemblance in question would not exist. Now, imagine that we were ignorant of the role of mimicry in survival and, despite Darwin's theory, could offer no explanation of why the resemblance to a snake existed in some places and not others. To use this failure as an excuse to say, "Well, God keeps changing his mind as to what he want caterpillars to look like" explains nothing. If some caterpillars looked like airplanes, we could say God wanted them to look that way.

Throughout most of human history, people had filthier habits than cats and dogs. Evolution suggests that we are descended from primates who, being tree dwellers, could let waste just drop to the ground. To say that God intended people to be filthier than cats and dogs, until recently when he changed his mind, is unsatisfying. If we discovered two-legged hedgehogs that ate iron, well God wanted there to be two-legged hedgehogs that ate iron. The same answer for everything, something that can "explain" anything, offers no scientific explanation at all. The whole point of science is to explain why things are this way rather than that.

To offer intelligent design in a science class as an alternative to Darwin is bad education. It impedes an understanding of what science is all about. It delights in any failure of science because that offers an opportunity to insert God into the gap. Who would teach any other subject in that way? No one who teaches engineering finds it useful to say that the reason a suspension bridge exists is that some intelligence designed it. The students want to know the principles of its construction, that is, how one builds a suspension bridge rather than an ordinary highway bridge. No teacher of engineering shouts with joy when he cannot say how some bridge was constructed. Such a teacher would be teaching anti-engineering rather than engineering. Intelligent design as a "science" is nothing other than anti-science.

The last word belongs to Jack Haldane (1892–1964), the great British biologist. When asked what his study of nature had revealed to him about God's purposes, he replied "an inordinate fondness for beetles" (quoted by Hutchinson, 1959).

Science and Values

Those untouched by religious faith sometimes emphasize the fact that science makes sense only if you have certain values. The argument runs as follows: values are subjective; science presumes certain values; therefore, science is subjective. There is a word of truth in this, but it does not really undermine the preferred role we give science in the search for truth.

Value-neutral people will not do science because value-neutral people will not do anything except sit frozen in a corner. Few people are like that, but some people have values that make them prefer pre-scientific notions about the universe, while others have values that make them prefer super-stitions like astrology. Many accept science eccentrically: they ignore only certain scientific theories, namely, those that conflict with something they value more like scripture or their views on race. Others still point out, correctly, that the practitioners of science may have unconscious or semi-conscious biases, love circles or favor men over women, that compromise their science. Even when witnesses in a courtroom think they are reporting things they saw, they may distort the truth.

However, as we have seen, enough people value science so that over the centuries we have got better and better approximations of reality. Most of us are glad of that, and if you are not, go on your independent non-scientific way. But you should recognize that in not valuing science, you pay an unusual price that none of you are willing to pay in a courtroom: getting as close to the truth as people with all their faults can. Although not value-neutral, science is a wonderful neutralizing influence and brings together those who respect it. I cannot force you to use a camera when you want to get as accurate a picture of something as possible. But if we do have a photo of the event, it can settle a lot of arguments afterwards. And astronomy takes a lot of photos that settle arguments about the heavens.

The fact that something is not universally valued in no way detracts from the fact that it is the best thing for doing a certain job, and in the case of science that job is to enhance human knowledge. The contention that science is subjective because personal bias distorts the practice of science is really a variant on a familiar contention: that science is sociologically relative, that is, reflects the biases characteristic of people in a particular culture at a particular time. We have already dealt with that. Whether personal or shared, bias makes for bad science, but reverence for the data is a corrective and a powerful one in the long run. I hope that I have convinced you that any prejudice you have against science will, to the degree that you entertain it, make you a worse critical thinker.

Corrupting the Youth

Confusion about science and history is divided between obscurantist churches and contemporary academics. The churches talk about "intelligent design" as an alternative science, and some university lecturers say, "reality is a text." The latter have less excuse for talking nonsense. The universities are fields on which a great battle rages. It is a contest pitting those who attempt to help students understand science, and how to use reason to debate moral and social issues, against those of whom it may be said that every student who comes within range of their voices is a bit worse off for the experience. It is up to the rest of us to point out the error of their ways, so that students can think clearly enough to filter their words and distil something of value.

Reference

Hutchinson, G.E. (1959) Homage to Santa Rosa or why are there so many kinds of animals? *The American Naturalist*, 93, 145–169.

Part 5
Nations and their Goals

18

Understanding Nations – Understanding Anyone

Key Concepts: (18) National interest; (19) national identity; (20) national affinities. *These three concepts are derived from three theories of international relations. Collectively, they offer spectacles that will help you discern the factors that affect the foreign policies of various nations.*

Preview: *Realism; liberalism; constructivism; realism revisited; the best pair of spectacles; common-sense psychology.*

I will begin with an analysis of the three main theories of international relations dominant today. As the introduction implies, I will borrow concepts from them all, rather than champion one over another, integrate the concepts borrowed, and make the psychology behind them explicit. In the next chapter, I will choose four examples of national behavior to see if our concepts illuminate them.

Realism

Realism, or neo-realism, perceives international relations as a competition between nation states. It sees a pattern in history: nations that ignore the balance of power and are unaware of their own interests usually pursue policies that benefit neither themselves nor others. As you can see, it does not claim that nations always pursue their interests. They may mistake or ignore where power lies, they may not perceive their interests or anticipate the consequences of their actions, and their internal politics may forbid doing what is best.

How to Improve Your Mind: Twenty Keys to Unlock the Modern World,
First Edition. James R. Flynn.
© 2012 John Wiley & Sons, Ltd. Published 2012 by John Wiley & Sons, Ltd.

Political realism does not deny that nations can seek to promote principles that transcend their interests, so long as their actions are not in conflict with the balance of power, and do not actually undermine their interests in a way that compromises their security. Other theories of international relations argue that the realist reading of history is too simplistic.

Liberalism

Liberalism, or neo-liberalism, argues that realism ignores an important lesson. The relative power of nations is sometimes less predictive of their behavior than whether or not they share culture, or are economically dependent on one another, or all have democratic government. Therefore, certain states at least need not look upon one another as potentially hostile actors and can pursue cooperative goals. The darker side of this is that states who lack the right culture or economic system or democratic institutions may be seen as dangerous.

Some construe this as meaning that democratic states have a mission to do nation building, that is, turn failed or dangerous states into better ones. However, liberalism's initial reading of history does not logically entail that conclusion. They are supplementary propositions whose truth must stand on their own merits. Attempts at nation building may be in fact almost impossible and counter-productive. If a society has not built itself into a viable state, it is unlikely that foreigners who are handicapped by ignorance and wishful thinking will do a better job.

Another supplementary proposition rests on a reading of very recent history, namely, that democracies do not fight one another. Therefore, weak democracies need not feel threatened by more powerful democracies and can often look to them for cooperation and aid. Most real democracies are a product of the twentieth century, and time will tell whether they will forego war with one another when faced with competition for oil and water. The French Revolution occurred over 200 years ago. But when Zhou Enlai, Premier of the People's Republic of China, was asked his opinion of its significance, he replied: "It's too early to tell."

No one should have any illusions about whether a democracy such as the US respects governments that have a democratic mandate and may be fledgling democracies. In Latin America, the US helped overthrow the democratically elected governments of Guatemala (President Jacobo Arbenz Guzmán) and Chile (President Salvador Allende). She thwarted popular movements in Puerto Rico, the Philippines, and Nicaragua. Since these were small and vulnerable nations, America could usually use subversion rather than hostilities that were recognizable as war. The exception was suppressing Emilio Aguinaldo in the Philippines, which took an all-out war lasting three years and cost many Filipino lives.

Nonetheless, the initial observation of liberalism is valid. There is no doubt that nations have natural allies who qualify because of an affinity of form of government, institutions, and interdependence. It is virtually unthinkable that, at least for the present, there should be a war between the US, Canada, Australia, New Zealand, any of the present members of the European Union (Turkey and Serbia are not members yet), Switzerland, and the Nordic states.

Constructivism

Constructivism sees another neglected message in history. Human behavior is often shaped by our sense of identity, and that is a product of our values, mores, culture, institutions, and history. Liberalism, with its sweeping categories like capitalism and democracy, misses the real role of shared ideals. Every state is a unique social construct capable of being transformed by the evolution of concepts and social practices. By ignoring this, realism often cannot account for a particular state's behavior, for example, America's commitment to Israel, which makes no sense in terms of America's interests or simply the fact that Israel is a democracy. The very existence of Israel is a product of Jewish identity.

Irish identity caused a war little remembered in America but well remembered in Canada. Immediately after the American Civil War, an Irish-American branch of the Fenians (who believed in armed struggle for Irish independence) launched an invasion of Canada. The purpose was to establish an Irish republic and trade Canada to the British for the independence of Ireland. Hundreds of thousands of Irish immigrants bought bonds to be redeemed six months after the recognition of Irish independence, and large quantities of arms were purchased. The Irish-American soldiers were mainly Civil War veterans. They sang:

> We are the Fenian Brotherhood, skilled in the arts of war; And we're going to fight for Ireland, the land we adore; Many battles we have won, along with the boys in blue; And we'll go and capture Canada, for we've nothing else to do. (see Box 18.1)

Box 18.1   The Irish invasion of Canada

They won some battles. In 1866, Colonel John O'Neill crossed the Niagara River (the international border) at the head of about 1000 men and briefly captured Fort Erie, defeating a Canadian force at Ridgeway. The invasion was broken when the US intercepted their supply lines and arrested 3000 reinforcements attempting to cross the river into Canada. The government purchased rail tickets for the Fenians to return to their homes if they promised not to invade any more countries from the United States.

This did not buy them off. In 1871, the Fenians lost a battle in Manitoba. Scouts spotted them almost immediately, thanks to a treacherous spy, and volunteer cavalry routed them. In the most exciting raid of that year, O'Neill captured a Hudson's Bay Company post thought to be in Canada but actually in US territory. Constructivism has proven its point. No identity other than Irish identity would have caused a war as strange as this.

There is no doubt that the nation sate is a social construct. Polar Eskimos have no concept of the nation state. They can comprehend killing for personal reasons but not a "war" in which you kill those who have done you no harm. The closest they can come is a sort of barroom brawl that gets out of hand. Genghis Kahn (1162–1227) did not think of his conquests as a political entity but as property to be divided among his heirs. The main asset was his army of about 130 000 men. He bequeathed 100 000 to his youngest son Tolui (as was traditional) and divided the rest among his other sons, mother, brothers, and the offspring of his sons and brothers.

Constructivism is too recent to call itself neo-constructivism, but there is a division between mainstream and radical constructivism. The latter rejects the belief that we can know external reality (whatever exists beyond one's own mind). They assert that the only reality we can know is whatever is represented by human thought and expressed in language, both of which are human constructs. We saw how silly this is in Chapter 14, and fortunately it is not true.

Human beings do paint word pictures of the world, but it is vital to distinguish between when these are approximations of reality and when they are excuses for not facing reality. For example, each of the nations of Southeastern Europe (what was once Yugoslavia) spins a history that makes

> ## Box 18.2   The green bullet
>
> Your kind of dictator is "a strong man". A full-scale war is a "police action". A bomb that takes out a whole building rather than half the neighborhood is a "smart bomb," and using it is a "surgical strike" (the medical profession has a good image). The innocent victims are "collateral damage. A "low-yield" nuke is a nuclear weapon that might kill only 10 000 people. My favorite is the "green bullet" that kills like any other bullet but, since it is not made of lead, does not pollute. I await the coinage of "happy homes" (where you kill everyone who refuses to go into a "strategic hamlet") and "Sweet William" (for a gas that kills everyone but leaves the foliage undamaged").

itself the victim and others the villains. An international group of historians is trying to identify historical events that any respectable historian must grant in an effort to make these nations give up self-serving myths. In other words, they are trying to replace language that creates fictitious history with language that captures what happened in the real world.

America has fallen into the rhetoric of a war on terror that precludes an objective assessment of who her real enemies are and alarms the rest of the world by its absurdity. The US military, and the military of most nations, uses attractive language to describe horrible weapons and actions in order to soften our perception of what they really entail (see Box 18.2).

Realism Revisited

What with all of these criticisms of realism, I want to say something positive. When analyzing the behavior of individuals, no one would ignore how much of it is self-interested. There is nothing wrong with this, and it certainly does not imply that people have no moral principles to which they sometimes sacrifice their interests. It is just that autonomous adults are expected to manage their own life, pursue their own career, mow their own lawns, raise their own children, and so forth. And when we pursue our interests, we try to establish a favorable balance of power.

In retirement, I am dependent on the decision-makers in my university to keep doing something I love, namely, giving two courses of lectures.

I want to foster good relations with my colleagues in my department and the head of my division, and, if possible, have an ally in the office of the President or Vice-Chancellor. If I know that if there is one negative person among the decision-makers who determine my fate, all the more important to have the others on my side.

But, as realism stresses, it would be mistaken to say that most people consistently seek what is actually in their own interests. They are led astray by ignorance and all of the psychological factors that affect human behavior: an exaggerated sense of self-importance, denial of their own limitations, lack of empathy, dogmatic morality, a sense of moral superiority, the primitive hunger to own land, the appeal of immediate over delayed gratification, the triumph of the pleasure principle over the reality principle (assuming the world is how you want it to be rather than how it is), the availability of displacement activities (activities that provide a convenient escape from the real world), romanticism (to be explained), and so forth. Later we will find this list useful in understanding why nations so often mistake what would achieve their goals.

Most nations are actors in an environment in which the pursuit of self-interest and power is more necessary, and therefore more excusable, than in the case of individuals. Most individuals operate in a society with a government that mitigates the ferocity of the struggle for power. The fact that nations and individuals differ in the degree to which they must be pre-occupied with power means a different balance between politics and ethics.

Politics favors the principle of "might makes right," and this is the antithesis of ethics. We can all appreciate how this balance alters. Honesty with loved ones admits of few exceptions (the main one is where the truth would be too wounding), honesty with neighbors admits of more exceptions, honesty in national politics must often give way to flattery (you want some vile member of parliament or congress to support a piece of good legislation), and a hymn of praise to a great power is sometimes necessary to protect the interests of a small state. You may even have to make sacrificial offerings of troops so a great power can hitch your flag to some disastrous adventure abroad. Even here, where the role of morality is at a minimum, it can dictate limits to dishonesty, so long as you do not face ultimate sanctions like conquest.

Moreover, while I will set aside speaking of the national interest in favor of national goals, the core interests of a nation state are easy to define: not being conquered by an alien people; reasonable maintenance of its prosperity: seeking allies who do not too much limit its autonomy. This does not always mean obsession with power but sometimes it does. When it does, states can be counted on to try to amass more power than rivals, if this is possible, and to gang up on a great power that clearly has imperialist ambitions, that is, they try to maintain a balance of power.

The Best Pair of Spectacles

I believe history has room for all three theories. No one can understand Finland without taking into account her fear of her powerful neighbor (Russia). No one can understand Israel without attention to her self-image. No one can understand why America has never conquered Canada without acknowledging the affinity between them as to institutions and values. Despite the obvious utility all have from one situation to another, the proponents of each tend to turn it into a world view, which, if not exclusively correct, is supposed to have a capacity to absorb what is valid in competing theories in a way the others cannot (see Box 18.3).

> ### Box 18.3   Alas, all academe
>
> When entering graduate study, American students are forced to commit to one school, or be consigned to the wilderness without a patron to guide them toward an academic post. Fortunately, they need only approach a (say) neo-realist professor and sell their soul: "Oh wise one, I thank God each day that you opened my eyes to the wickedness of constructivism and liberalism. I will take your courses and forsake all others, if you will only accept me as an acolyte." In 1952, when I began graduate study at Chicago, there were charismatic professors, but I recall no such pressure to commit. Perhaps at the tender age of 18, I was clueless but I would like to think that things were not so crazy in those days.

I am going to create some "trifocals," that is, spectacles that combine the strengths of the three theories. In order to see through them:

(1) *Posit a nation's goals* (realism). Sometimes a goal qualifies as part of its core national interest, sometimes not. Usually you can find goals that are so clearly desired as to be beyond dispute.

(2) *Describe the nation's identity* (constructivism). Here, the emphasis is on the subjective, that is, less on the total national character than on its image of itself.

(3) *Make a list of affinities* (liberalism). Name the nations that are natural allies based on mutual appreciation of one another's culture, behavior, or institutions; also name those that are natural enemies based on historical animosities or conflicting ideologies.

Common-Sense Psychology

We would not neglect any of the factors the various theories identify when analyzing the behavior of an individual. We say of a person sometimes he seeks his interests in so far as his power allows; sometimes he treats his friends as such rather than as mere means to his ends; sometimes you have to take into account his image of himself as a person with elevated morals. This gives us hope of success. A caveat: human and international behavior has a complexity that sometimes defies analysis. There are cases in which more complicated spectacles are useful. But it is surprising how far a simple pair can take us.

19

Four Cases – Making Sense Out of Nonsense

Key Concepts: (18) National interest; (19) national identity; (20) national affinities when combined into a pair of spectacles. *The spectacles may sound good in theory, but do they actually work? Do they actually illuminate the behavior of nations that otherwise seems puzzling?*

Preview: *Why does Israel ignore its national interest?; Israel's identity; the shadow of the holocaust; why does America support Israel?; America's national interest; America's identity; American exceptionalism; why did imperial Spain make an unconditional commitment?; why did Britain seize the Suez canal?; an audit.*

To show that our spectacles illuminate the behavior of all nations would require another book. I will demonstrate their utility by selecting four examples that pose difficult problems of explanation. They are all cases in which nations seem relatively blind to their national interest. But they differ as to the lessons they teach. Israel and America are blinded by self-image. Imperial Spain illustrates how a great power took on too many commitments. Britain and Suez shows how a great power in decline refused to face the fact that it could no longer behave with impunity.

The Case of Israel

Posited goal: Maximize Israel's chances of survival
Identity: savior of Jewish people and their culture; a minority believe they are
    God's chosen people with a mandate to restore Israel's biblical boundaries.

How to Improve Your Mind: Twenty Keys to Unlock the Modern World,
First Edition. James R. Flynn.
© 2012 John Wiley & Sons, Ltd. Published 2012 by John Wiley & Sons, Ltd.

Natural allies: America
Natural enemies: the Islamic world, particularly the Middle East
Neutral: most of the rest of the world

Israel's National Interest

From 1948 (the war of independence) to 1967 (the Six-Day War), Israel did what any other nascent state would have done. She defeated her enemies when they attacked her and built up a military establishment (including nuclear weapons) that made her superior to all the Arab states combined.

In 1967, Israel acquired territory on the West Bank of the Jordan River and control over all of Jerusalem. From this point forward, she had to choose. She could slowly absorb all of the West Bank that was desirable (arable) and count on an eternal military advantage over Arab states whose hostility was guaranteed by her expansion. Or she could say to herself: the modernization of the Middle East is inevitable, and Arabs will get their own nuclear weapons and build modern armies. Therefore, we need to demonstrate to the world, particularly to the Arab world, that we have limited territorial ambitions; and that we will promote a viable Palestinian state on the West Bank as a concession to Palestinian nationalism. There is no guarantee that this will be acceptable, but it offers the best chance of eventual tolerance of our existence.

There is a minority within Israel that wants her to adopt the second path toward survival. I think they are correct. But the point is that when arguing my case, I must do so in terms of the concept of Israel's national interest. And since I think the choice is clear, I must explain why Israel cannot perceive her national interest. The same is true of those who disagree (how is it that I am so blind to Israel's interests?). The point is not that you must agree with me but about what I must discuss to make my case plausible.

I believe that absorbing the West Bank does nothing to serve Israel's long-term security: whatever portion of it she absorbs will do nothing to protect her from being overwhelmed should modernization occur. Moreover, it tends to alienate the US, the only potential ally that, thanks to its own military advantage over the rest of the world, could cancel out Arab military superiority. Why then has Israel turned her back on the second option?

Israel's Identity

Some of the reasons that obscure Israeli thinking about her interests apply to all states. Both Israel and the Arabs feel that they win the blaming game, the game of saying who did what to whom and who was most wicked. There is the primitive nationalism that delights in annexing more and more land. There is the appeal of immediate gratification over distant deferred gratification. Every Israeli wants the impossible, namely, for the violence to stop now. The evacuation of the Gaza strip has been a great trauma. Rather than a peace dividend, Israeli got a hostile government next door and an escalation of violence. A short-term reverse arouses emotions that no long-term and problematic benefit can match. There is a ready-made displacement activity: one can conduct so-called peace negotiation and shut one's mind to the fact that they have no chance of success so long as the expansion into the West Bank continues.

Other factors reflect Israel's peculiar history and national identity. First, there are orthodox Jews who believe that the Jews are God's chosen people with a mandate to restore Israel's biblical boundaries. They see the West Bank as belonging to Israel by Divine command, and rush in to settle its land whether the government actively aids them or simulates a feeble opposition. Second, the majority of Israelis tend to have a romantic image of the settlers. In the early days, all Jews admired the settlers as heroic people morally superior to themselves. They were the frontiersmen of Zionism, sharing hardship and reward with an equality to which we all pay lip service, and with the Calvinist virtues of hard work and frugality that Americanized Jews admired. Third, Orthodox Judaism preserved Jewish identity throughout centuries of dispersal and persecution. Many atheists attending reform synagogues acknowledge in their hearts a historical debt.

The Shadow of the Holocaust

Now, we face the greatest mystery of all: why does Israel go out of its way to gratuitously insult America?

In May of 2009, President Obama "demanded" a halt to the expansion off settlements because he saw this as a major obstacle to the establishment of an independent Palestinian state. The next day, Israeli government spokesman Mark Regev said that the Prime Minister (Binyamin Netanyahu) would defy the White House by continuing construction in existing settlements. Obama responded by suggesting that Israeli intransigence endangers America's security. Israel did not comment. In March of 2010, in order to promote peace negotiations, Vice-President Joe Biden arrived in Israel to be confronted with an announcement that Israel will build 1600 new Jewish housing units in predominately Arab East Jerusalem. Secretary of State Hillary Clinton telephoned Netanyahu to express "frustration." Netanyahu later expressed regret over the timing of the announcement but gave no indication it would be rescinded.

One hypothesis: the shadow of the Holocaust. Western nations closed their borders to Jews trying to escape Hitler. Who have the Jews ever been able to trust but themselves? Think of the psychological price of a conscious admission that Israel's future is dependent on the goodwill of a gentile state. Think of the need to prove that Israel is self-sufficient, that she can afford to defy her patron, even though such defiance verges on the suicidal.

A like-minded Jewish scholar tells me this omits something about Jewish identity: their history has simply made them unwilling to take orders from others. There is certainly a contrast between their behavior and that of America's other client state Taiwan. Despite the stereotype of the non-Chinese as barbarians, Taiwan has never defied the US so openly. Whatever the solution to this mystery, one thing is certain: the concept of national interest is a prerequisite to explaining the behavior of nation states, but it is not sufficient.

Why Does America Support Israel?

Posited goals: preservation of Israel and amicable relations with the Islamic world

Identity: American exceptionalism or the belief that the US is untainted by the vices of the Old World

Natural allies: Europe and Australasia by cultural affinity; Japan with a reservoir of goodwill from the occupation and as a protectorate; Israel by cultural affinity and as a protectorate; Taiwan as a protectorate

Natural enemies: Latin America due to a history of intervention; the Islamic world, particularly the Middle East, due to a history of intervention and unconditional commitment to Israel

Ambiguous: India and Pakistan because America vacillates between them; Russia due to recent great power rivalry; China because of support of Taiwan with the complication of economic interdependence; Sub-Sahara

Africa alienated by the status of black America but sees the election of
Obama as a sign of progress
Neutral: practically no one except perhaps the Polar Eskimos

America's National Interest

US interests are fatally compromised by Israel's expansion into the West
Bank. It tarnishes America's image throughout the Islamic world,
particularly in the Middle East with its oil wealth. Time after time, US
Presidents have stated the obvious, namely, that they wanted Israel to at
least freeze the number and size of settlements on the West Bank. The only
trend over time is that Israeli Prime Ministers have gone from tactful
temporizing to immediate public statements that the US can go fly a kite.
Whoever heard of a great power that allowed a client state to treat it with
such contempt? Obama's Fiscal Year 2010 budget includes $2.8 billion in
military aid for Israel. America could terminate aid unless Israeli policy
alters but never does so.

There are two problems that require explanation: why does America
support Israel at all; and why is American support so unconditional?

America's Identity

A very small part of the explanation of America's support is the American
political system. The method of electing a President is that each state has
electoral votes roughly in accord with its population, and these votes are
awarded on the principle of winner takes all. US voters are about evenly
divided between the two major parties, so it is vital to win big states like
New York and Florida, and get their large blocs of electoral votes. Also,
campaigns are expensive to finance. Jewish Americans are concentrated in
these states and do much to subsidize campaigns.

America's identity is far more important. The Bible permeates the
American consciousness. This creates a presumption that the land of Israel
in some sense belongs to the Jewish people. However, the Bible does not
mean much to most American intellectuals, and their stance is crucial.

America's intellectual elite has its own peculiar mix. I refer to the ties of
affection and mutual respect between US intellectuals and American Jews,
one that, for its intensity, is historically unique. Non-Jewish intellectuals

marry Jews, have close friendships with Jews, interact with Jewish colleagues, and know how much poorer the US cultural scene would be without them. They have friendships with other minorities of course, but these are not minorities whose history of persecution is so manifest, whose very existence was recently threatened by a lunatic, whose whole history and identity are bound up with a foreign nation state. It becomes unthinkable to tell Jewish Americans that the state of Israel is at risk.

Foreign policy is unlike domestic policy. It is formulated by opinion elites, which is to say by American intellectuals. So, explaining why America supports Israel at all is easy. Explaining why America is so tolerant of the price this entails is more difficult.

American Exceptionalism

America is in denial about what support of Israel entails. This has deep roots in America's image of itself. I refer to "American exceptionalism": the belief that America is a unique social experiment free of the corruption that taints other nations. Since America feels morally secure in its own conscience about Israel, it finds it hard to take contrary opinion seriously. After all, Israel is an American ally; its people have a place in American hearts; and its government resembles American democracy. American, American, American – clearly to be American is to be something very special. The presumption is that America has the right to act unilaterally because its motives are pure. The fact that America's commitment to Israel is unacceptable to the Islamic world just shows how flawed the Islamic world is.

Some realism is in order. American support of Israel can be absolute in the sense that America's commitment to Japan and Iceland is absolute. They are treated as if they were part of American soil, with all of America's might as a deterrent to anyone who might threaten their existence. But American support cannot be absolute in the sense of being unconditional. It should be conditioned on the integration of the West Bank into a viable Palestinian state. The long-term persistence of America's present commitment is suspect precisely because it may in the long run extract too great a price. The real alternatives are between an unconditional commitment likely to expire, and a conditional commitment likely to persist. Israel will never get a timeless guarantee that it is secure. No nation has ever got that: history never guarantees anything.

Other Lessons from History

We will look at two more cases of international behavior that teach us something about the limits of military power when it ignores the real world. One concerns a great power that pursued an unconditional commitment to the brink of disaster and finally had to abandon it. The other concerns a former great power that did not appreciate the extent to which political power is based on economic power.

An Unconditional Commitment: Spain and the Netherlands

Posited goal: possession of the Low Countries (Holland and Belgium) for the sake of Catholicism and as a source of wealth
Identity: defender of the faith
Natural allies: Austria (the Hapsburgs)
Natural enemies: Ottoman Empire, France, Britain, Holland, Protestants in general

The Catholic faction in the Netherlands had an unconditional commitment from the greatest power in the world. Philip II of Spain said, "I would rather lose the Low Countries than reign over them if they ceased to be Catholic." That Spain would honor this commitment seemed guaranteed by the fact that she was heavily dependent on the Netherlands to maintain her own solvency. Antwerp was the center from which gold and silver bullion from the New World was distributed, and its financiers were experts in raising loans. As for Spain's military might, her Tercios were by far the best professional troops in Europe.

Nonetheless, the Eighty Years War (1568 to 1648) levied a price that Spain eventually found too heavy to pay. The North of the Netherlands (Holland) was Protestant, and the South (today's Belgium, Luxembourg, and French Flanders) was Catholic. Spain's commitment to domination by the Catholic faction alienated all of the Protestant areas. There was also a general perception that Spain would seek to exploit the wealth of the Netherlands as long as she held sway. Spain was initially successful in suppressing the rebellion. However, in 1572, the Protestants captured Brielle, and the rebellion gained momentum. The northern provinces became independent in fact, although this was not recognized until much later.

Her commitment in the Netherlands was one too many. From 1571 to 1585, Spain fought against the Ottoman Empire. In 1588, she sent her Armada to conquer Protestant England and lost her fleet. She had to rebuild it to transport gold and silver from Spanish America to Spain and protect her ships against privateers licensed by other nations. From 1590 to 1598, Spain intervened in the religious wars in France. Although defeated she did help ensure that France would remain Catholic. After 1598, her military presence in the Netherlands (on France's northern border) was disastrous. It ensured that France would remain an enemy, Catholic or not. France entered the war on the side of the Dutch. In 1643, in the Battle of Rocroi, she defeated the Spanish, whose infantry hitherto had been considered invincible. In 1648, Spain finally recognized Dutch independence. By 1659, Spain was unable to defend itself against France and ceded her both Artois and southern Flanders.

The morale of the Spanish people was shattered. After 80 years of an unwinnable war, they saw higher taxes, a ruined economy, and their sons dead, with nothing to balance the scales. Spain's decline as a great power dates from that time.

Homily: History never repeats itself, and no one would argue that Catholic versus Protestant in the Netherlands was identical to Israel versus the Islamic world in the Middle East. For one thing, the Catholic population was not composed of recent settlers, and Protestants did not dispute its right to exist. Therefore, even when Spanish-Catholic efforts to dictate the economic and political future of the area failed, Catholics were not eliminated but presented with a partition that was acceptable. There was an obvious boundary between the two factions that could command respect from all. The Catholics of what later became Belgium remained under Catholic Spain. Catholic France annexed the others.

But it does show that even the most committed great power cannot persist when its commitments are out of touch with political and economic reality. It took 80 years for political reality to wear the Spanish down. America has arguably been even less realistic than they. She invaded Iraq, one of the few Arab states in the Middle East that systematically hung those who might threaten the US with terrorist attacks. She has attempted to pacify Afghanistan. If Pakistan goes fundamentalist, can it be far behind? She has shown the world how easily her military power is exhausted, even when she confronts no great power. As for the wealth of the area, her present policy is perfectly designed to make access to oil difficult.

Money and Power: Britain and Suez

Posited goal: recover control of the Suez Canal and overthrow Egyptian regime

Identity: former great power undergoing nervous breakdown over loss of status

Natural allies: France and Israel

Natural enemies: the nations of the developing world and, therefore, America who was competing with the USSR for their goodwill

Britain appreciated neither that the days of colonialism were over nor that she was no longer a great power, able to act independently where the interests of a real great power were involved. President Nasser of Egypt annoyed Britain by his policies in the Middle East and annoyed the US by buying arms from the Soviet bloc. America withdrew aid to build the Aswan Dam, and Nasser responded on July 19, 1956 by nationalizing the Suez Canal. Britain made a secret military pact with France and Israel that aimed at regaining the Canal. On October 29, 1956, Israel attacked Egypt, and her troops conquered the Sinai Peninsula. Six days later, British and French troops went into action and rapidly secured the Canal.

The US was castigating Soviet suppression of the Hungarian revolution of 1956 and found itself expected to endorse Western intervention to overthrow a leader of the developing world. Eisenhower told Britain that unless she withdrew, he would sell the US reserves of British currency and thereby undermine the value of the pound (today, China is in a position to do this to the US). This would have meant that within weeks, Britain could not import the food and energy needed to sustain her population. On November 6, 1956, the British and French agreed to withdraw all of their forces.

Even after Suez, Britain could not give up the illusion of playing the role of a great power. She now enhances her self-esteem by claiming a "special relationship" with the United States that is supposed to allow her to influence US policy. This causes great amusement in Washington, because it means automatic support from Britain for a negligible price, a bit of flattery and having to endure editorials in *The London Times* about the need to correct American brashness with English wisdom.

Homily: In 1909, when imperial Britain was still intact, it would have seemed incredible that by 1956, a mere 47 years later, she would be humiliated by an economic veto. How long before America finds that economic interdependence with China will force her to coordinate her policies with

China as an equal? Given the recent economic crisis, the year 2056 may be too optimistic a forecast.

One thing we know: America will not hold her own by bundling debt into pieces of paper. There is no global issue from the environment to oil to control of weapons of mass destruction that is not dependent on future cooperation between America and China. Everything else is a distraction from the great goal of turning their interdependence into mutual regard and confidence in one another's probity.

An Audit

The three concepts borrowed from theories of international relations cannot confer omniscience. You would need to know everything worth knowing about every state that exists and many non-state actors as well. A more reasonable objective is to select from history what is most relevant to assessing American foreign policy (because America's actions and fate affect everyone) and that of your own nation.

It is unlikely that more than an elite will ever learn enough to assess their nation's foreign policy. Even when the general public becomes uneasy, it takes dissidents from the policy elite (former generals are particularly useful) to convince the public that the government's call for patriotism is hollow. The fact that opinion elites are so influential should please you. If you become informed enough to argue a case, you join a select group of discussants and are not lost in the mass public.

The concept of the national interest will never be superfluous. It is priceless, because it allows for a non-moralistic debate. People find it even harder to agree about morals than they do about what is in their interest; and moral appeals across national boundaries almost always run aground on every nation's assumption of its own moral superiority. Bertram Russell was a strong moral advocate. But he said that he would be joyful if only people would really pursue their interests rather than folly. Nine times out of ten, if nations did what was in their interests, their policies would be much less destructive and lamentable than they are.

20

Conclusion
Gene Debs University

The 20 Key Concepts are steps toward transcending our time through comprehension, so that you can do more than live out your life as its unreflective creature. If you are about to go to university, you will find that some of your lecturers rave like loons, but now you know why and can learn from them nonetheless. You can also learn from your reading lists and the university library. And now you can profit from what you read because the information will be organized by an orderly mind.

Some of those who read this book will be university lecturers, and they may protest that their universities offer a broad education and that many of their students have accumulated the conceptual tools they need to confront the modern world. I suspect that they are mistaken. As evidence, I offer the example of Gene Debs University. This is a fictitious name for one of America's great state universities. It was kind enough to allow a sample of its senior class to take Flynn's Index of Social Criticism (FISC). They got a full report. Here, I just summarize the essentials.

Sample and Test

Within two months of graduation, members of the senior class were solicited by email and offered $12 to give an hour of their time. Majors from four areas were targeted: Economics, Business, Mathematics; the social sciences; the humanities; and the natural sciences. The number who took the test was 185 or 3.22% of the senior class (no. = 5739). One student took

How to Improve Your Mind: Twenty Keys to Unlock the Modern World,
First Edition. James R. Flynn.
© 2012 John Wiley & Sons, Ltd. Published 2012 by John Wiley & Sons, Ltd.

it twice, apparently motivated by avarice. The average GPA of the sample was 3.41 as compared to 3.29 for all seniors.

The fact that the sample was slightly elite did not affect the results. One of the most disturbing findings was that GPA was virtually uncorrelated with performance on the FISC at 0.06. The traits that earn good grades at Gene Debs University do not include critical ability of any broad significance.

There are 20 items, which are divided into four subtests: elementary market analysis and the ability to apply the concept of a ratio (Economics subtest); social science methodology sufficient to be wary of flawed studies (Social Science subtest); flawed argument including some of the classical errors philosophy has identified (Philosophy subtest); and the role and status of science including natural science, history, and social science (Science subtest).

Each item presents five alternatives, and the student must identify the two that are more reasonable responses than the remainder. Taking a class as a whole, I have put the standard for acceptable competence on an item at a score of 1.40. If 40% of the class could identify both of the correct responses, 30% one correct response, and the other 30% were just guessing, they would get an average of 1.415. Or if half knew the two correct responses, and the other half knew nothing, they would get 1.40.

Class competence by item

Box 20.1 conveys the content of the FISC items and gives the average performance on them. It shows that these near-graduates have reasonable mastery of the concept of a placebo and can detect a tautology (circular reasoning). They are close to competence concerning the relativist fallacy (arguing that all values are relative and then making an arbitrary exception) and the practical syllogism (perceiving that both a moral principle and a fact are necessary to reach a moral conclusion).

Awareness of the need for a control group is weak and ability to use the law of supply and demand variable by major. They have only random opinions about whether nature has purposes (it does not). They are unable to apply the concept of a ratio or percentage. They are unaware of the charisma effect and do not understand the concept of a random sample. They are unaware that you cannot settle a moral debate by an appeal to nature (homosexuality is unnatural) but stop short of the foolishness of endorsing butter as more natural than margarine. They have only random opinions about the role and nature of the sciences.

Box 20.1 The FISC and Gene Debs

The FISC items and concepts: student performance ranked from best to worst.

Concept	No. of items	Scores (0.8 = random; 2.0 = maximum)	Comment
Placebo	1	1.42	Competence
Tautology	1	1.42	Competence
Relativist fallacy	1	1.38	Close to competence
Practical syllogism	1	1.34	Close to competence
Control group	1	1.26	Minority competence
Law supply/ demand	3	1.15	Variable competence by major
Purposes in nature	1	1.06	Opinions close to random
Ratio	2	1.04	Cannot apply
Charisma effect	1	1.01	Unaware
Random sample	1	0.96	Unaware of its nature and virtues
Natural = good	1	0.81	Unaware of fallacy of
Butter = natural	1	1.47	equating natural with good, but stop short of butter is good because it is "more natural"
Science unique	1	0.97	Random as to whether
Scientific history unique	1	0.62	science and the historical method are reliable, and
Social science and bias	1	0.78	as to whether social science can transcend bias
Sociologist's fallacy	1	0.39	Unaware that equating for one factor often entails non-comparability for another
Universe blank slate	1	0.25	Believe no interpretation of reality more objective than any other

They are prone to commit the "sociologist's fallacy" (unaware that matching two groups for one variable can produce a mismatch for another), but that is a rather subtle concept, and scholars of considerable seniority do no better. They are prone to deny reality as a check on opinion, which relates to their lack of competence to talk about science coherently. This does not mean, of course, that biology majors would think that what they find in the laboratory is not to be preferred to ordinary opinion. It is just that they have not generalized from what they do as scientists to reach conclusions about science itself.

Student Competence by Subtest

To be credited with high competence in a particular subtest or area, the student had to achieve a score of 7.0 out of a possible 10. This is just 1.40 (the single item standard) times five items. About 17% of Gene Debs graduates are competent in basic market analysis and use of ratios, 22% in basic social science methodology, and 29% in rational discourse. I suspect that the detection of flawed argument is higher because a really bright person can come closer to doing this unaided. So, Gene Debs has a lot of bright students. Almost nine out of 10 of its graduates have no coherent view of science of any sort: 2.70% are consistent realists; 8.65% are consistent postmodernists; the rest vacillate randomly between the two. That less than 3% of graduates really know what science is all about is depressing.

Majors and Divisions

The fact that some departments fare better or worse may not reflect on the performance of their academic staff. There is no sign that any department attempts to develop other than narrow critical competence; or, if they do, it is not reflected in GPAs. The seven majors I will discuss had 12 or more students in the sample, and unless a follow-up is done with larger numbers, caution is in order.

(1) Economics: The benchmark to which others should aspire. It stands first on the Economics subtest with its average student at least approaching competence. Its students are not as strong on social science

methodology as they should be. Its students are competent at detecting flawed argument (Philosophy subtest). Given that a bright student can develop this skill without much formal training, variations between majors on the Philosophy subtest may largely reflect differences in the quality of their students.

(2) Political Science: Almost equal to Economics. It is surprising that its majors come as close to economists on market analysis, but perhaps a lot of them take the introductory macroeconomics course. A bit better than Economics on social science methodology, but no major has a good grasp of this.

(3) History: Bright students, but it is disturbing that its majors have only minimal competence on social science methods.

(4) Neurology: Stronger than expected on social science methods but does not approach functional competence on any subtest.

(5) Psychology: Surprising lack of competence in social science methods.

(6) English: No real critical competence outside its special field.

(7) Biology: No critical competence outside its special field. Despite being a science, among those few with a coherent vision of science, more lean toward postmodernism than toward realism.

There were only six Business majors, but their GPA was above average. They were worst or next worst in every area including Economics. If these six students took Macroeconomics during their freshman year, they were not interested.

Conclusions

- Gene Debs university has a senior class with many bright students.
- No effort is made to develop their critical competence outside narrow specialties.
- No more than 24% of their graduates have found their own way to a reasonable level of wide critical competence (at least two areas out of four).
- Only about 3% of their students have a coherent realist image of science, while almost 9% are at least attracted to a post-modernist concept.
- Apparent differences in critical competence between various majors are large and disturbing, and these should be tested against further data.

Box 20.2   Mongo

In the film, *Blazing Saddles*, there is a character named Mongo who is a brutish, virtually subhuman cowboy. He rides a Brahmin Bull, and when a horse gets in his way, he hits it on the jaw and knocks it out. When asked what he thinks the future holds for him, he says: "Mongo not know. Mongo just a bit of flotsam floating on the great tide of history." Certainly, we can do a better job with our students than that. Those who wish to administer the FISC at their university or high school can contact the author: jim.flynn@otago.ac.nz

Every university worthy of the name believes that its graduates, whatever their specialties, should have the common good of a liberated mind. Therefore, they have programs called the "core curriculum," or the "general education requirement," or the "great books," or what have you. At present, these are opiates that dull our awareness of what we all know: no university educates as well as it pretends. The Key Concepts are there, but students cannot see them for what they are; they disappear in a sea of knowledge that drowns their significance (see Box 20.2).

James Mill

James Mill, the father of John Stuart Mill, believed that universal literacy would be enough to cure all the ills of humankind. I have no such illusion about what this book offers. There will never be a time when everyone wants to think critically. Thinking critically has never been an automatic ticket to power. But those who do equip themselves with the Key Concepts will enjoy the kind of liberated mind without which no true personal autonomy is possible. No longer like patients etherized on a table, young men and women, fully aware, can rise to confront the world and do what can be done to make it into an imitation of the good.

Index

How to Improve Your Mind: Twenty Keys to Unlock the Modern World,
First Edition. James R. Flynn.
© 2012 John Wiley & Sons, Ltd. Published 2012 by John Wiley & Sons, Ltd.

Index

Index